ON THE EVE OF THE MILLENNIUM

*The Future of Democracy
Through an Age of Unreason*

CONOR CRUISE O'BRIEN

MARTIN KESSLER BOOKS

THE FREE PRESS

New York London Toronto Sydney Tokyo Singapore

The Free Press
A Division of Simon & Schuster Inc.
1230 Avenue of the Americas
New York, NY 10020

First American Edition 1995
Printed in the United States of America

printing number
1 2 3 4 5 6 7 8 9 10

Library of Congress Cataloging-in-Publication Data

O'Brien, Conor Cruise
    On the eve of the millennium: the future of democracy through an
age of unreason / Conor Cruise O'Brien—1st. American ed.
        p.   cm.
    Originally published: Don Mills, Ont.: House of Anansi, 1994, in
series: CBC Massey lecture series.
    ISBN 0–02–874098–X (hard). — ISBN 0–02–874094–7 (pbk.)
    1. Civilization, Modern—1950– 2. Christianity and culture.
3. Enlightenment. 4. Democracy. 5. Catholic Church—Relations—
Islam. 6. Islam—Relations—Catholic Church. 7. Catholic Church—
Doctrines. 8. Sex—Religious aspects—Catholic Church.   I. Title.
CB428.027   1995   95–35636
303.49'09'05—dc20   CIP

"The Second Coming" by William Butler Yeats is reprinted with the per-
mission of Simon & Schuster, Inc., from *The Poems of W. B. Yeats: A New
Edition,* edited by Richard J. Finneran. Copyright 1924 by Macmillan
Publishing Company, renewed 1952 by Bertha Georgie Yeats.

Contents

I
THE
ENLIGHTENMENT
AND ITS ENEMIES

I SHALL BEGIN WITH one of W. B. Yeats's most famous poems, "The Second Coming."

Turning and turning in the widening gyre
The falcon cannot hear the falconer;
Things fall apart; the centre cannot hold;
Mere anarchy is loosed upon the world,
The blood-dimmed tide is loosed, and everywhere
The ceremony of innocence is drowned;
The best lack all conviction, while the worst
Are full of passionate intensity.

Surely some revelation is at hand;
Surely the Second Coming is at hand.
The Second Coming! Hardly are those words out
When a vast image out of *Spiritus Mundi*
Troubles my sight: somewhere in sands of the desert
A shape with lion body and the head of a man,
A gaze blank and pitiless as the sun,
Is moving its slow thighs, while all about it
Reel shadows of the indignant desert birds.
The darkness drops again; but now I know

That twenty centuries of stony sleep
Were vexed to nightmare by a rocking cradle,
And what rough beast, its hour come round at last,
Slouches towards Bethlehem to be born?

The rough beast that Yeats expected, around the end of the First World War, would have been a mystical force assuming a political shape, whether of Communist or Fascist colour, and moving through the blood-dimmed tide to dominate a new post-Christian Era. By our own time, the rough beast has divested itself of those particular colours, but Yeats's images have lost nothing of their relevance. Mere anarchy is loosed upon huge areas of the world, and the blood-dimmed tide is loosed in more than fifty wars in the middle of the last decade of the second millennium of the Christian Era. For us, too, Yeats's question remains a haunting one:

And what rough beast, its hour come round at last,
Slouches towards Bethlehem to be born?

I shall come back to that question. But first I should like to look at how people thought and felt a thousand years ago, on the eve of the close of the *first* millennium of the Christian Era. As it happens, the most arresting description we have of these matters is from the pen of the great French historian, Jules Michelet, in the section devoted to "The Year 1000," in his monumental *History of France*. As well as being a great historian, Michelet is also a great master of French prose. As with all great masters, his prose suffers greatly in translation. His account of the year 1000 has far more impact in the original ardent and idiosyncratic French than it can possibly have in any translation. I propose, therefore, to read Michelet on the year 1000 in takes, first in the original and then in translation:

> Cet immense concert de voix naïves et barbares, comme un chant d'église dans une sombre cathédrale pendant la nuit de Noël, est d'abord âpre et discordant. On y trouve des accents étranges, des voix grotesques, terribles, à peine humaines; et vous douteriez quelquefois si c'est la naissance du Sauveur, ou la Fête des fous, la Fête de l'âne. Fantastique et bizarre harmonie, à quoi rien ne ressemble, où l'on croit entendre à la fois tout cantique, et des *Dies iræ* et des *Alléluia*.

A translation of that opening would read:

> This vast concert of naive and barbarous voices, like the chanting in a sombre cathedral during Christmas night, seems at first harsh and discordant. You find strange accents there, grotesque voices, scarcely human, and you would wonder sometimes whether this was the Birth of the Saviour, or the Festival of Fools, the Festival of the Donkey. Fantastic and bizarre harmony, to which nothing can be likened, and in which you think you hear simultaneously every kind of canticle, *Dies iræ* and *Alléluia*, all being sung together.

"Birth of the Saviour," "Festival of the Donkey." Strange anticipation there, though in a less scary mode, of Yeats's rough beast, slouching towards Bethlehem to be born.

After that baroque overture, Michelet continues in a more analytical manner:

> C'était une croyance universelle au moyen âge, que le monde devait finir avec l'an 1000 de L'Incarnation. Avant le christianisme, les Étrusques aussi avaient fixé leur terme à dix siècles, et la prédiction s'était accomplie. Le christianisme, passager sur cette terre, hôte exilé du ciel, devait adopter aisément ces croyances. . . . Ce monde ne voyait que chaos en soi; il aspirait à l'ordre, et l'espérait dans la mort. D'ailleurs, en ces temps de miracles et de légendes, où tout apparaissait bizarrement coloré comme à travers de sombres vitraux, on pouvait douter que cette réalité visible fût autre chose qu'un songe. . . . Il eût bien pu se faire alors que ce que nous appelons la vie fût en effet la mort et qu'en finissant, le monde . . . *commençât de vivre et cessât de mourir.*

Translated:

> It was a universal belief in the Middle Ages that the world would end with the year 1000 from the Nativity. Before Christianity, the Etruscans had fixed the term of their civilization at ten centuries, and the prediction had been fulfilled. Christianity, a transient on earth, an exile from heaven, was to adopt the Etruscan term. . . .

This world saw nothing in itself but chaos; it longed for order and hoped to find it in death. Besides, in those times of miracles and legends, where everything appeared in bizarre colours, as if through dark stained glass, people could doubt whether this visible reality were anything other than a dream. . . . It could well be that what we call life was really death, and that by ending, the world . . . began to live and ceased to die.

Michelet goes on:

Cette fin d'un monde si triste était tout ensemble l'espoir et l'effroi du moyen âge. . . . L'empire romain avait croulé, celui de Charlemagne s'en était allé aussi . . . et ils continuaient. Malheur sur malheur, ruine sur ruine. Il fallait bien qu'il vînt autre chose, et l'on attendait. Le captif attendait dans le noir donjon . . . le serf attendait sur son sillon . . . le moine attendait, dans les abstinences du cloître, dans les tumultes solitaires du coeur, au milieu des tentations et des chutes, des remords et des visions étranges, misérable jouet du diable qui folâtrait cruellement autour de lui, et qui le soir, tirant sa couverture, lui disait gaiement à l'oreille: "Tu es damné!"

In English:

This end of such a sad world was at one and the same time the hope and the horror of the Middle Ages. . . . The Roman Empire had gone, that of Charlemagne also . . . and suffering continued. Misfortune on

misfortune, ruin on ruin. There must be something else
to come, and people were waiting. The prisoner waited
in his dark dungeon . . . the serf in his furrow. . . . The
monk waited in the abstinences of the cloister, in the
solitary tumults of the heart, in the midst of temptations
and of remorse and curious visions, miserable
plaything of the Devil who fooled around him cruelly
and who, at night, pulling back the bedclothes would
say gaily into his ear: "You're damned!"

Ten centuries separate us from the people whom
Michelet describes. In terms of history, this is a very
long span. Those people lived halfway between our
own time and that of the early Roman Empire, the time
of Jesus Christ. But in biological terms, in terms of the
existence of our species on earth, a thousand years is
as nothing. Those people, our ancestors, were very like
us indeed. They were smaller, because less well-fed,
and the information available to them was different.
That's about all.

You may think that the "all" is quite enough, since
it includes a huge difference in beliefs. But the difference is not so huge as those of you who are children of
the Enlightenment may think. There are actually *more*
people in contemporary North America who believe
in the literal truth of the New Testament's *Book of
Revelation* than there were in medieval Europe who
believed the same. (There are more, because there are
more of *all* sorts of people.) And it is of course on the
Book of Revelation that the expectations about which
Michelet writes are founded. St. John, in *Revelation*,

tells us that Christ will return to earth and reign for a thousand years. After that, Satan will again revolt, but will be crushed and cast into the lake of fire and brimstone there to be tormented day and night forever and ever (*Revelation* 20.10). After that comes the new Jerusalem, seen by John in the twenty-first chapter. I shall now quote the first seven verses of that chapter:

> And I saw a new heaven and new earth: for the first heaven and the first earth were passed away; and there was no more sea.
>
> And, I, John, saw the holy city, new Jerusalem, coming down from God out of heaven, prepared as a bride adorned for her husband.
>
> And I heard a great voice out of heaven saying, Behold, the tabernacle of God is with men, and he will dwell with them, and they shall be his people, and God himself shall be with them, and be their God.
>
> And God shall wipe away all tears from their eyes; and there shall be no more death, neither sorrow, nor crying, neither shall there be any more pain: for the former things are passed away.
>
> And he that sat upon the throne said, Behold, I make all things new. And he said unto me, Write: for these words are true and faithful.
>
> And he said unto me, It is done. I am Alpha and Omega, the beginning and the end. I will give unto him that is athirst of the fountain of the water of life freely.
>
> He that overcometh shall inherit all things, and I will be his God, and he shall be my son.

I pause there, on the seventh verse. "He that over-cometh shall inherit all things . . ." That is the promise that buoyed up Martin Luther King and his companions and followers when they sang "We shall over-come. . . ." This is the most notable example of the millennial spirit at work in the twentieth century. It is, obviously, a benign example. But the vision of St. John is also charged with menace. The verse that immediately follows "He that overcometh shall inherit all things . . ." runs as follows:

> But the fearful, and unbelieving, and the abominable, and murderers, fornicators, and sorcerers, and idolaters, and all liars, shall have their part in the lake which burneth with fire and brimstone: which is the second death.

The message of *Revelation*, whether consoling or menacing, is not confined to Christianity. It is also part of Islam, which claims to complete it. Muhammad, like St. John, wrote at the dictation of an angel, and death on earth, as well as the second death, is the penalty for refusal of the angelic message.

Of course you can believe in *Revelation*, and therefore in the Second Coming, without necessarily believing that the Second Coming will happen in the year 2000. After the failure of the hopes, fears and expectations for the year 1000, Christian fundamentalists have to be a bit more cautious. Yet there is a general notion that the date must have a solemn, sacral significance. Pope John Paul II is known to feel this. It is his earnest wish that his pontificate shall extend to the close of the second millennium of the Christian Era. He clearly hopes to be able to deliver an encyclical of epochal importance in the year 2000. And in preparation for that, he has reason to believe that he is already working with epochal and world-transforming forces.

Pope John Paul II, on the eve of the chronological millennium, feels himself to be at the centre of the emergence of a spiritual millennium, in which the religious of the world will be united for a final victory over the irreligious. He has helped to bring about, for certain limited purposes, initially at least, an alliance between official Catholicism and fundamentalist Islam. The startling and paradoxical nature of this alliance has itself a tang of the millennium about it. The alliance was formed in defence of a perceived threat to common traditional values, in the matters of sexuality and reproduction. The agenda of the Cairo Conference on Population and Development in September 1994 was felt to infringe these common values, in relation especially to abortion and contraception (homosexuality was also targeted, for reasons whose relevance to the Cairo agenda was less obvious). Vatican statements tended to limit the alliance to these particular topics, but some of the Islamic fundamentalists, in Iran and Libya, were more far-reaching in their statements in the run-up to Cairo. They envisaged a world-wide alliance of the religious against the irreligious, the righteous against the unrighteous. The heirs of the crusades and the heirs of the *jihad* uniting for a final war against the godless.

This general concept has undoubtedly been attractive to Pope John Paul. The idea of an Alliance for the Repeal of the Enlightenment is most congenial. The last quarter of the second millennium of the Christian Era (from 1500 to now) has been a time of disaster for the Catholic Church, bringing with it first the Protestant Reformation in the sixteenth century and then, even worse, the Enlightenment, in the seventeenth and eighteenth centuries. At one time, indeed, it might have seemed that there was a bright side to the Enlightenment, even from a Catholic point of view. On the whole, the Enlightenment affected countries that had embraced the Reformation, more deeply than Counter-Reformation countries. France, which had embraced neither Reformation nor Counter Reformation, but whose people were generally classed as Catholic, was the only country which the papacy, by the late eighteenth century, had cause to regard as "lost" to the Enlightenment. And that indeed was a major loss: the Church had lost her Eldest Daughter. But up to the second half of the twentieth century, adherents of the papacy could regard the Enlightenment with some complacency, seeing it as a terminal disease of Protestantism, and, as such, a merciful manifestation of the inscrutability of Divine Providence.

But in the last quarter of our century, such complacency became no longer possible. It became clear that the rot had set in in the Vatican's own backyard. I state the phenomenon in the terms in which the papacy perceived the spread of Enlightenment values among the faithful. By around 1975, it became apparent that the *Magisterium* — the supreme authority of the papacy in matters of faith and morals — was no longer working, even among those Catholics with the greatest traditional reputation for obedience to the leader of the Church. For the Catholic Church, as an institution, there was no field of morals that was more sensitive and significant than that of human sexuality and reproduction. Within that field, there was no Catholic doctrine that was more distinctly and firmly articulated than the total prohibition of recourse by the faithful to artificial means of contraception. Up to near the end of the third quarter of the twentieth century there was clear evidence that the faithful were still obeying the instructions of the Church. Catholic families were significantly larger, and often *much* larger, than other families. But by the 1970s, the differential was shrinking, and by the 1980s, it had vanished altogether, in certain traditionally Catholic countries and regions.

The critical areas were those in which there were sizeable populations which were both traditionally Catholic, and sufficiently educated and informed, in a worldly sense, to avail themselves of artificial means of contraception, should they decide to defy what they knew to be the unequivocal and peremptory teaching of their Church. Two such areas were French Canada and the Republic of Ireland. And by the 1980s it had become clear that Canadian and Irish Catholic married couples were deliberately disobeying the solemn and reiterated instructions of their Church regarding sexual and reproductive ethics. From a Vatican point of view, this meant that the wolf of the Enlightenment, having devoured Protestantism, was now at large in the sheepfold of the True Church itself.

When I refer to the influence of the Enlightenment, I don't, of course, mean that the Catholic couples who decided to disobey the instructions contained in *Mater et Magistra* (1960), *Humanae Vitae* (1968), and other papal and episcopal documents did so because they had been poring over the works of Locke and Montesquieu, of Voltaire and Diderot and d'Alembert. Quite possibly most of the Catholic couples concerned, in Canada and Ireland, for instance, had never heard of any of those thinkers or even, perhaps, of the Enlightenment itself. Nonetheless, these men and women show, by the nature itself of their decisions, that their minds are thoroughly permeated by Enlightenment values, no doubt acquired through the wider Protestant and post-Protestant environment of the British Isles and of North America. They have made rational decisions, based on their understanding of their own personal situation, as to what would be best for their own happiness on earth as married people, and for the happiness of their children. They have stuck to those decisions in the teeth of peremptory orders to the contrary, supposedly based on divine and revealed authority. These are classic Enlightenment positions, and when they have been adopted by so many Catholics, the sum of all those decisions represents a massive erosion of the papal *Magisterium*, through the permeation of Enlightenment values. And the erosion and permeation don't stop there. Once you have disobeyed one solemn in-junction, supposedly of divine inspiration, you are likely to disobey any of the other injunctions that seem to you unreasonable. Most Irish Catholics today seem disposed to reject the Church's teaching on divorce and are divided about its teaching on abortion. Among Canadian Catholics, if I understand aright, the process is even further advanced.

In the Third World, birth and fertility rates among Catholics remain satisfactory, from a papal point of view. But the papacy cannot derive much satisfaction from those statistics. The Pope knows that the figures reflect lack of information about, and access to, meth-ods of contraception, rather than obedience to papal encyclicals. John Paul II, however, is prepared to settle for denial of information and access, if he cannot get obedience. To secure such denial has been the basis of Vatican policy in the field of sexual and reproductive ethics at every relevant international conference in the second half of this century, culminating in the Cairo Conference on Population and Development.

This is in many ways an awkward policy for the Catholic Church in the modern world, and many Cath-olics greatly resent it. It is a policy which gives the Church a vested interest in the preservation of igno-rance. It puts the Church back on the road of confron-tation with the mainstream Enlightenment. Around mid-century, with the processes of thought that led to Vatican II, the Church had seemed to be coming to terms with that Enlightenment. But the present Pope, with formidable pertinacity — and an ingenuity which has seemed hardly less formidable until very recently — has managed to repeal Vatican II in spirit, while piously preserving the letter of all its documentary formulae. And beyond that, the objective is nothing less than the repeal of the Enlightenment itself. John Paul hopes and prays that the opening of the third millennium of the Christian Era will be the turning point in the battle against Enlightenment values. And he hopes, as he has told us, to be presiding over the destinies of the Catholic Church when that great turning point is reached.

If the Pope has his way, and if his successors persist in that way, the state of mind of humanity, towards the end of the third millennium of the Christian Era, will be more like that of the medieval French towards the end of the first, as described by Michelet, than like the state of mind of the advanced world as it is today, on the eve of the close of the second.

Let me pause here to take a breath as we contemplate the scale and time span of that colossal project. I frankly abhor Pope John Paul II. Hardly a day passes that I do not murmur to myself the prayer contained in the seventh verse of the psalm "Deus Laudem." That was the prayer François Villon applied to his own bishop, whom he hated. The verse runs: *Fiant dies eius pauci et episcopatum eius accipiat alter.* "May his days be few and may another receive his Bishopric." Yet, though I abhor him and hope to see the end of his pontificate — *before* the close of this millennium — I cannot withhold a meed of grudging admiration for the scope of his grand design, and the energy and tactical craftiness which he has devoted to its fulfilment. That said, I am wholeheartedly on the side of those who wish to frustrate that design.

My central subject matter in these discourses is the future of the Enlightenment. I understand that as comprehending also, within itself, the future of democracy, freedom of expression, and the rule of law. That statement needs to be qualified, for the rule of law is anterior to the Enlightenment, as commonly understood. Magna Carta dates from the thirteenth century, not the eighteenth. Also the rule of law applies not only in post-Enlightenment societies but also in societies where Enlightenment values by no means prevail. The rule of law can even operate *against* Enlightenment values. It was the rule of law, in the France of the *ancien régime*, that required heretics to be tortured to death. If a humane and/or enlightened prince tried to stop that, he would be told by the *Parlement* that the law was above him and required such punishment. That was why Voltaire and others preferred enlightened despotism to the rule of law. It was a reasonable preference under the conditions of the *ancien régime*. Similarly, the rule of Islamic law — the *Shari'a* — operates, wherever and however it is enforced, to the exclusion of practices based on Enlightenment values.

In Western societies, however, where the laws themselves have been shaped and tempered by centuries of Enlightenment values (or by imitations of laws so shaped, as in the case of non-Western countries like Japan), the rule of law, associated as it is in these societies with democracy, freedom of expression, and market freedom, is inseparable from the general heritage of the Enlightenment.

How secure is that heritage? I think not all that secure, for reasons I shall be discussing. Most of those reasons are within the Enlightenment heritage itself. They are strong enough to cast some doubt over its survival to the end of the next century, let alone the virtually unthinkable end of the next millennium. But let us first consider the threat that has been most conspicuous in recent times, which comes from outside the Enlightenment itself. It takes the form of what I have called the Alliance for the Repeal of the Enlightenment: the making of common cause, for certain purposes, by official Catholicism and fundamentalist Islam.

This alliance can be made to sound more formidable than it actually is. Thus, some Muslim enthusiasts for this "war of the religious against the irreligious" have been speaking as if the alliance represented two billion people: one billion Catholics and one billion Muslims. The exaggeration is wild. Most of these people have never heard of any such alliance, and are not aware of what their supposed representatives are saying on their behalf. Many Muslims are not fundamentalists, and many of these are much more afraid of fundamentalist Islam than they are of contraception, abortion, and Western values. Many, indeed, want as much access to Western values and information as they can get, and resent the Islamic fundamentalist insistence on denial of that access, wherever Islamic law prevails, or can be made to prevail.

On the Catholic side, most Catholics are probably only dimly aware of what the Vatican is up to internationally. Of those who are aware, probably a majority is opposed. Almost all of the many Catholics, both religious and lay, who work or have worked among the poor in the Third World bitterly resent what they regard as the intransigent and obscurantist papal line on the ethics of sexuality and reproduction. I know one eminent and erudite Catholic authority on population problems who never refers to the present Pope otherwise than as "that fellow."

Among Western Catholics not directly concerned with Third World problems there is not, and cannot be, any enthusiasm for this aspect of papal policy. These Catholics do not, in their personal lives, accept their Church's teaching on sexuality and reproduction, so how could they support the attempt to impose these values on other people? In practice, they neither support this attempt nor oppose it. They just ignore it, or try to do so. A pity; their overt opposition to this project could stop it.

The attempted alliance with Islam, over reproductive ethics, has to be unpopular with Western Catholics. The publicity about the Vatican's overtures to Iran and Libya, in August 1994, was embarrassing to the Vatican and disturbing to Western Catholics, especially American Catholics. A Libyan spokesman, on the eve of the Cairo Conference, suggested that the Vatican position on the Lockerbie terrorist bombing is supportive of Libya. Some good Catholics, normally not inclined to ask questions about the Head of their

Church, must have begun to wonder exactly what is going on out there in the Vatican these days when they read *that* little news item from Tripoli.

It is still too early to say whether the attempted alliance between official Catholicism and fundamentalist Islam that emerged on the eve of Cairo will be of lasting significance. The Vatican would wish it to be so, if it can be conducted with the degree of discretion customary to the conduct of the Curia. This may be hard to achieve. Rome likes the zeal of its new Islamic allies, but the style that goes with the zeal can be a little unnerving. And not only the style; some of the activities also.

Islamic fundamentalists, as well as being anti-contraception, anti-abortion, anti-homosexual and anti-Jewish, are also addicted to what the decadent West describes as terrorism. This makes them uncomfortable allies for sedate Roman clerics who are themselves more affected by the Enlightenment values which pervade Western culture than they would like to think, though less than the rest of us might wish. Rome is living, however queasily, in the twentieth century. The Islamic fundamentalist allies are robust and uninhibited denizens of a medieval intellectual world. That the said denizens have oil money to spend on explosives makes them even more dicey as allies of the Curia.

On the whole, however, I think some kind of Catholic-Islamic alliance is likely to subsist at least for the duration of the present pontificate. As long as the papacy remains committed to the principles of *Mater et Magistra* and *Humanae Vitae*, and to the implementation of those principles wherever possible, it is going to need those Islamic allies. And it is precisely the characteristics that make the allies embarrassing that make them also indispensable. The line of thought here is not peculiar to the Church of Rome. The Pope is a prince and any prince may affect to deplore the ruthlessness of an ally while being privately aware that the ruthlessness is what makes the ally so desirable. This is the sort of thing Machiavelli understood so well and blurted out to the ruin of his career, and to the infamy of his reputation. John Paul II understands these things just as well but will never blurt out anything. The circumspect can be just as ruthless as the candid, and often more effectively so.

Rome is committed to the prevention of the dissemination in the Third World of information about contraception and safe abortion. States under the control of Islamic fundamentalists, such as Iran, will see to it that such information is kept out of the areas where their writ runs, and that those who attempt to bring it in are severely punished. But also wherever there are large Muslim populations, as in the Indian subcontinent, Islamic fundamentalists will do what is necessary to prevent the spread of such information, irrespective of the views of the regime they live under. They will burn down abortion clinics and beat or kill abortionists. They will investigate married couples with suspiciously small numbers of children and punish those whom they find guilty of abortion or contraception. (Incidentally, traditional Islam does not appear to have been opposed to contraception, but modern Islamic fundamentalists are violently opposed to it as contrary to Islam. Actually, anti-contraception among Muslims appears to be an import from the West, probably via Rome.) In general, Islamic fundamentalists (like some Jewish and Christian fundamentalists) punish women who show outward signs of Western-style emancipation — as by wearing dress regarded as immodest — or who are believed to have practised or countenanced abortion or contraception.

Islamic resistance to the spread of Enlightenment values and practices involves various levels of violence. For women, in particular, it involves a constant, implicit threat of violence, combined with frequent exposure to actual violence: a sort of quiet reign of terror. The actual violence employed, in countries not actually under an Islamic-fundamentalist state regime, would be regarded by Westerners as lawless, and is almost certainly so regarded by the law in the countries of residence involved. It is not so regarded in Islam. For Islam it *represents* the rule of law: the only valid law, that of Islam. If the government, in any of the regions of divided Islam, fails to uphold and enforce Islamic law, then pious male Muslims have the right and the duty to enforce it, and to administer appropriate penalties to their womenfolk, and to any males who try to lead their womenfolk astray.

The Vatican could never publicly condone the violent methods by which Islamic fundamentalists resist the intrusion of secular values and practices. But it has made itself an accessory to these methods by seeking an alliance with the Islamic fundamentalists, precisely because of their resistance to those values and practices.

The Vatican's alliance with Islam is likely to continue. But it will assume more discreet forms. Direct contacts with terrorist regimes will be avoided. There will be no more special missions to capitals like Teheran and Tripoli. Direct contacts with Islam will be with countries which are religiously conservative but cultivate good relations with the West. Saudi Arabia is the most obvious case in point.

On the eve of the Cairo Conference the government of Saudi Arabia announced its decision not to participate. Appropriately, it was the Saudi religious authorities who explained the government's decision. The country's most senior religious figure is Sheikh Abdul-Aziz bin Baz. The sheikh issued a *fatwa* proclaiming that the agenda for Cairo, which had been approved by the United States and other Western countries, "will encourage promiscuity, homosexuality and equality for women" and therefore had to be condemned. The Vatican cannot openly applaud the third objection of the Saudi divine. Yet we may be sure that a warm message of general approval for the *fatwa* has winged its way from Rome to Riyadh. Pope John Paul II cannot feel altogether happy about how much more powerful a *fatwa* is than an encyclical, in the late twentieth century. Yet the Rome-Riyadh Axis is a fact and ranks among the principal achievements of the Counter-Enlightenment papacy.

As far as effects on the West are concerned, the Vatican's new alliance is doing more harm to the Catholic Church than it does to the heritage of the Enlightenment.

In particular, this union subjects the Vatican's relationship with the United States to severe strain. Most Americans dislike what they know of Islamic fundamentalists, because of their perceived addiction to terrorism and their claim to jurisdiction — including the infliction of the death penalty — in non-Islamic countries, as well as in Islamic ones. In addition, the alliance has confirmed and enhanced the perception of the Catholic Church as hostile to women. That hostility had seemed evident, not merely from the Vatican's policy on abortion and contraception, but also from its position on women as priests and its defence of the monopoly of power, within the Church, enjoyed by celibate males. The Islamic alliance revealed these positions to rank so high within the value system of the Roman Catholic Church as to become the basis of a reconciliation between that Church and a creed known from its foundation to be fundamentally hostile to Christianity for refusing to accept the Koran.

In so far as John Paul II's aim is the repeal of the Enlightenment in the West, the particular issues on which the Church has chosen to make a stand appear singularly ill-chosen. Where the ethics of reproduction are involved, the vital interests of most women are involved in resisting the Church's project. George Bush's alliance with the Vatican in the name of family values was high among the reasons why Bill Clinton was elected president of the United States. And that is why the United States was able to confront the Vatican at Cairo.

At Cairo the Vatican was aligned against the U.S. in

an attempted partnership with some regimes which are bitterly hostile to that country. Nor did Vatican tactics, over Cairo, do anything to mitigate that confrontation. Departing from traditional Vatican suavity and obliquity, the Vatican spokesman made a personal attack on the head of the U.S. delegation, Vice-President Al Gore. In general, the trend of Vatican rhetoric, in furthering the "increase and multiply" doctrine of Genesis and *Mater et Magistra*, has sought to fan Third World hostility against the West. The troubles of the Third World, so the Vatican argues, are not due in any measure to the so-called population explosion but entirely to the selfishness and greed of the capitalist West in exploiting their resources.

The Vatican has not yet got round to calling the United States the Great Satan, as its Iranian allies do, following the teaching of the late Imam Khomeini. But the Vatican's rhetoric is more congenial to the Great Satan theorists than anything that can be heard from any other Western source.

The Cairo Conference was itself a fiasco for the Vatican. The Islamic allies were a broken reed, as far as the conference was concerned. Many of them — including the wily Saudis — simply stayed away, regarding the gathering as so evil in nature that it would be a sin to attend it, even in order to combat its godless agenda. This was a characteristic Saudi position, combining the appearance of extreme Islamic austerity with the pragmatism of avoiding confrontation with the United States. An Iranian delegation did go to Cairo, but seems to have been under the control of the pragmatic President Rafsanjani rather than of the fanatical Ayatollah Khamenei. In any case, it failed to follow the Vatican in challenging documents co-sponsored by the United States and Europe. By the end of the conference, the Vatican was at the nadir of its international influence, totally isolated and widely unpopular. The conference ratified the positions it had opposed.

As far as Catholic influence in the West is concerned, the policies of John Paul II culminating in the wooing of fundamentalist Islam have been an unmitigated disaster. The Vatican's onslaught has worked to confirm, rather than to undermine, Western commitment to Enlightenment values. When the Vatican summons fundamentalist Islam to its aid, the heirs of the Enlightenment can see how precious their heritage is, by the measure of the forces arrayed against it and still dominating large and populous regions of the globe.

The Vatican can find some consolation for its failure in the West, when it contemplates the Third World. The Vatican cannot, at least as yet, shake the Enlightenment, in Western heartlands, but it can arrest, or at least delay, the diffusion of these values, and of practices associated with them, in the Third World. The quite recent conversion of fundamentalist Islam to the anti-contraception cause has been an important specific victory. And in general, the approval of the Vatican has lent an aura of international respectability, somewhat lacking previously, to the Islamic fundamentalists. This helps them in their struggle against their secular enemies, who are also the Vatican's enemies.

More important even than respectability is the factor of triumphalism. Fundamentalist Islam believes in the imminent triumph of Islam throughout the entire world. The fact that the Pope — the greatest ayatollah of the West — is now seeking to make common cause with Islam is an evident harbinger of the triumph to come.

The Christian faith is regarded by Muslims as an incomplete, and partly incorrect, version of their own. What is needful is that those who are now Christians should accept the message that God dictated, through his angel, to the Prophet Muhammad. Islamic fundamentalists believe that that conversion is imminent. What more fitting than that it should come at the close of the second millennium of the Christian Era, thus closing that era, once and for all, and ushering in one that would see the terrestrial and universal triumph of the House of Islam?

Theodor Herzl, in the days before he became a Zionist, dreamt of the mass-conversion of the Jews to Catholicism: a conversion presided over by the Pope, in Rome, to the ringing of bells. Might not the Pope, in the year 2000, announce his acceptance of the Koran and summon the faithful, through the papal muezzin, to join him in prayer in the Mosque of St. Peter?

Personally, I should think such an event quite unlikely. But then all previous generations, both of Catholics and of Muslims, would have thought *any* kind of alliance between the papacy and Islam exceedingly unlikely.

When the Pope made overtures to Muslims noted

for their piety, he must have appeared, in Muslim eyes, to be taking a long step in the direction of Islam itself. Why might not Allah, in his Mercy and Compassion, guide the Pope to take the decisive step: the acceptance of the Blessed Koran? What Muslim could set limits to the Mercy and Compassion of Allah?

By stimulating such reflections, the papal wooing of Islam boosts the morale of the Islamic fundamentalists and shakes the foundations of every secular regime throughout the Muslim world. And that is precisely what John Paul II aims to do. The idea that he may be about to embrace Islam is one that serves to advance the purposes of his pontificate. He is the Pope of the Counter Enlightenment as surely as any of his six-teenth- and seventeenth-century predecessors were popes of the Counter Reformation. John Paul II is not about to embrace Islam. But he is not averse to giving the impression that he may be about to do so, by stressing the values which Catholicism shares with Islam. The notion of his possible conversion to Islam serves the holy cause of the Counter Enlightenment.

I should like to revert to my opening topic: Michelet's picture of Christian expectations at the end of the first millennium. There is a paradox here.

We on the eve of the close of the second millennium have reason to feel less remote from the contemporaries of the close of the first than Michelet did, a hundred and thirty years ago. Michelet, in the 1860s, was an exuberantly confident child of the Enlightenment, of whose early and universal triumph he entertained no doubt. Evil was essentially part of the dark past. It was a fruit of the superstitions whose sway he describes in his account of the year 1000. *Le temps des Messianismes est passe!* he cried. The time of Messianisms is past!

It would be hard for a thoughtful person, in the late twentieth century, to share that superb nineteenth-century confidence and optimism. We are separated from all that by two world wars, by Gulag and the Holocaust. We know that Messianisms *can* return. It was the Messianism of the Dictatorship of the Proletariat that gave our century Gulag. It was the Messianism of the Biological Revolution that gave us the Holocaust. Our century has known horrors exceeding in scale all the horrors of the preceding centuries, great though those horrors were. And since the end of the Second World War, people have had to live with the idea of the end of the world through thermonuclear war as a real and imminent possibility.

So apocalyptic ideas are not utterly strange to us children of the twentieth century, as they were to nineteenth-century thinkers like Michelet. Our century has known anguish of apocalyptic dimensions. Even those of us who are children of the Enlightenment have to feel more akin to the men and women who lived in anxious expectation of the year 1000 than thinkers of the eighteenth or nineteenth century could possibly feel. Our cosmology is different from that of those ancestors, but our psychology is much the same.

Here I had better stop generalizing for a moment and speak for myself. I feel myself to be a child of the Enlightenment, but a somewhat chastened and battered one. Partly this is a mechanical result of having lived a long time. It is what Edmund Burke called "the late ripe fruit of mere experience." Specifically, this is a result of having lived through most of the twentieth century, from its second decade to its last. Most of the great crimes of our century were perpetrated by people — Communists and Nazis — who regarded themselves as thoroughly emancipated from the superstitions of the past. They sacrificed human beings by the millions in the service of pseudo-scientific doctrines devised by aggressive and over-confident intellectuals.

The Enlightenment we need is one that is aware of the dark, especially the dark in ourselves. An Enlightenment that is on guard against hubris. An Enlightenment that is aware that there is far more evidence extant in favour of the Christian doctrine of Original Sin than of Rousseau's doctrine of Original Virtue. An Enlightenment that respects the religious imagination, but not the claim of some religious to know what God wants from us and to have the duty to enforce that knowledge.

An Enlightenment, finally, that knows that even the enlightened have to sleep and that our dreams are not particularly enlightened. They can be, indeed, quite like the dreams of Michelet's poor monk, with that frolicsome devil whispering in his ear, "You're damned!"

In a novel called *The Bertrams* published in 1859 — the same year as Darwin's *Origin of Species* — Anthony Trollope wrote: "The bodily attendance of the devil may be mythical; but in the spirit he is always with us."

When my son Patrick was aged eight, he asked me a question: "Daddy, do you believe in ghosts?" It was a beautiful sunny morning on the Hill of Howth, and I was that much younger then, and more confidently enlightened in proportion. So I answered: "No, Patrick, of course not." Patrick replied: "Yes, Daddy, that's how I feel, too. All the same . . . when you're up in the attic . . . in the dark . . . and you hear those little feet-feet coming after you . . . sometimes you'd wonder."

You might indeed.

II
DEMOCRACY AND POPULARITY

IN THIS CHAPTER I WANT TO CONSIDER, on the eve of the millennium, democracy, popularity, and freedom of expression, the relations between them, and possible futures for them, jointly or separately. But first a word about the idea of "on the eve."

There is a famous novel of that name by Turgenev, written in the 1860s. It was a kind of holy book for Russian intellectuals on the eve, as they thought, of a great and liberating revolution in the Russian Empire. The characters in the novel believed that, and so did the Russians who loved the book, quoted it, and almost lived it towards the end of the nineteenth century and for about a decade and a half of the twentieth.

These Russians had indeed been living on the eve of a Russian revolution. But the revolution that happened wasn't anything like the one most of them thought was coming. They had also, though very few of them had at all been aware of this, been living on the eve of the First World War. Even Lenin, the most farsighted, and among the most hard-hearted, of the Russians in question, found it difficult to believe in the coming of European war. He did indeed understand that Russia's involvement in war, and Russia's backwardness as compared with other European powers, would provide unprecedented opportunities for a revolutionary movement, about whose character he and his close associates had no illusions. But when the chain of events that led to the war was set in motion by the assassination of Archduke Franz Ferdinand at Sarajevo, Lenin was sceptical: "I cannot believe that Franz Joseph and our Nikolashka will give us that pleasure."

Pleasure: Russia's revolutionary destinies were now in the hands of a man who thought of the coming of the First World War as a pleasure. And it was precisely because he was sufficiently hard-hearted and ferocious to think and feel along those lines — and had surrounded himself with like-minded and like-hearted people — that he and his friends would prevail amidst the horrors that accompanied and followed the collapse of the Russian armed forces in 1917.

In the early 1920s, at a time when Bolshevik power had come to dominate almost the whole of the former Russian Empire, a now-forgotten Russian poet thought bitterly about Turgenev's *On the Eve*. He contrasted the expectations on the eve with the realities of the day. He wrote: "We who are sons of Russia's dreadful *day* . . ."

That line is a salutary reminder to those who, like me, have the nerve to talk and write about "on the eve" of anything, that we never know what we may be on the eve of. We can indeed predict anniversaries. We know that the second millennium of the Christian Era will come to an end in a certain year which most people think of as the year 2000. There is no need for us to argue with those who tell us it is really 2001. It is the round thousands that have the magical power; that goes back to the ancient Etruscans and the ancient Jews. Around these cluster the magical hopes which we call millennial or chiliastic. These have certain psychic resonances even among people who consciously think of themselves as secular and rational. Among believing, traditional Christians, the resonances will necessarily be stronger. Pope John Paul II, if his health sustains him, will be preparing himself for signs in the year 2000, and for some apocalyptic announcement on his part at Easter of that year.

The year 2000 is now less than five years away. We can form an approximate idea of what the conditions in our society and on our planet will probably be like in that year. We expect those conditions to be quite like those we know in 1994, and we are probably right. We have to bear in mind, however, that we could be terribly wrong. Conditions in the second half of 1914 were very different indeed from those experienced in the second half of 1909. True, the positions of the European powers were sufficiently established, and Balkan insecurity sufficiently alarming, to have aroused, by 1909, fears of war. In 1994, on the other hand, although Balkan insecurity is much worse that it was in 1909, there is little or no fear of a general European war. The almost universal feeling is that the threat of a general war was extinguished by the collapse of the Soviet Union. This is probably so, and for a longer period ahead than what remains of the present century and millennium. Yet even within that very short period, there are ugly possibilities whose fulfilment we cannot exclude, even within the next five years. Conditions in the former Soviet Union, including the leakages of nuclear material and technology, suggest what some of these possibilities may be. They include: nuclear blackmail by a future Russian government, activated by a combination of ultra-nationalism and acute economic distress; nuclear weapons in the hands of rogue states, like Iran and Libya, followed by nuclear blackmail from those quarters; nuclear weapons in the hands of terrorists, followed, again, by nuclear blackmail. And, in any of these cases, the existence of the nuclear capacity could involve its demonstration by the detonation of a nuclear device.

Any of these possibilities could become a reality within the next five years. In fact, all three of them might. And if any of them does — still more, if all do — conditions in the year 2000 will be very different from the relatively comfortable and secure conditions that most of us in the West are now enjoying.

In parenthesis, I presume that Western governments and security establishments are preparing countermeasures to meet all of the eventualities I have listed. The confidence and speed with which Western countries are pursuing disarmament might give the contrary impression. I hope this is misleading and that the countries concerned are, in secret, redeploying defensive measures to meet new threats of a different order to those envisaged throughout most of the second half of this century. I hope that this is so, but I don't have sufficient confidence in the wisdom of late-twentieth-century Western governments simply to assume that this is the case. The experience of the last few years permits us no such confidence, either about dealings with rogue states or with terrorists.

As regards the former, we have had the case of Iraq. By the summer of 1992, Saddam Hussein was openly threatening to invade Kuwait. A clear warning from Washington, that the United States would treat such an invasion as a direct threat to its interests and a hostile act, would probably have prevented that invasion. Instead, what Saddam received in late July, through the American ambassador in Baghdad, was a clear message that America regarded the dispute as an inter-Arab affair. So Saddam went ahead with the invasion. Nobody but a fool could have expected him to do anything else.

How many other fools are there around now, dealing with Iran, for example?

Nor does the posture of the American government towards my own particular national brand of terrorist, the Irish Republican Army, in the second half of 1994, encourage any confidence in its capacity to cope with terrorist blandishments or terrorist blackmail. On 31 August 1994, the IRA announced what it called "a complete cessation of military operations." This was in fact an open-ended tactical ceasefire, within a strategy that still aims at the destabilization and eventual annexation of Northern Ireland. The IRA, still intact as a private army and in possession of an estimated 100 tons of weaponry, will use the ceasefire period for progress towards these aims in a number of ways. It asks Dublin and Washington to put pressure on London to "respond" to its "complete cessation of military operations" with "peace dividends," meaning a series of concessions to the IRA, envisaged as leading, within a few years, to the destruction of Northern Ireland. Failure to provide the "peace dividends" would be seen as "endangering the ceasefire." Dublin and Washington fell in with this line and became in effect allies of the IRA (*aka* Sinn Fein) for the duration of the ceasefire.

The loyalist ceasefire, six weeks after the IRA one, is based on the assumption that "the Union is safe," meaning that Northern Ireland's position as part of the United Kingdom is now secure. But the IRA and Sinn Fein made it clear that, unless Northern Ireland ceases to exist, the IRA will resume its military operations at a time of its own choosing.

The present double ceasefire is therefore not a stable peace, but a most fragile truce, based for the present on contradictory political assumptions by the two parties to the ceasefire.

Meanwhile, in Northern Ireland, the IRA pursued its own agenda of destablization. The chosen agency for this purpose, under ceasefire conditions, is what is known as "the unarmed strategy," the substitute for the armed struggle for as long as the ceasefire lasts. It consists of street protests and acts of civil disobedience, beginning sporadically and escalating to massive mob violence (but short of "military operations"). The immediate objective is to infuriate the Protestant population, provoke renewed violence on the part of the loyalist paramilitaries, and preferably bring about confrontation and collisions between these and the security forces. At some point in this process, the IRA can get out its — still readily accessible — guns, and resume military operations, in defence of the Catholic people. The longer-term objective is to make Northern Ireland ungovernable and thereby bring about British withdrawal. This will be followed by civil war in all Ireland between Catholic and Protestant, and by ethnic cleansing, Bosnian style.

Both Dublin and Washington, for their own political reasons, are ignoring all the copious danger signals, and are following the Sinn Fein line that the IRA announcement means "peace," and that all people of goodwill must do everything in their power to preserve the "peace" in question. This means putting pressure on the British to make concessions to the IRA and to keep on making concessions to them.

The Clinton Administration needed the peace — or rather, the perception of peace — to last up to November 8 and the American Congressional elections. The attainment of peace in Northern Ireland could be seen, in the run-up to those elections, and during them, as a major achievement of the president's in the field of foreign policy and therefore a strong reason for voting for the Democratic ticket.

The president, of course, has competent analysts and advisers who could have told him, if he was listening, that the IRA announcement of 31 August 1994 does not mean peace, or anything like it. But the president was not interested, in the autumn of 1994, in advice about the actual situation in Northern Ireland. He was interested in how a version of that situation could be packaged and presented in order to enable Democratic candidates to win as many seats as possible.

On his way back from the Cairo Conference, U.S. Vice-President Al Gore touched down at Shannon Airport, where he had a half-hour meeting with Taoiseach Albert Reynolds, and talked to the press. This was a week after the IRA ceasefire and the day after Reynolds gave a press conference in Government Buildings, Dublin, along with Gerry Adams and John Hume. Vice-President Gore told the press how greatly he admires Reynolds, and also that Ireland was now "at the top of the U.S. foreign policy agenda."

I didn't feel altogether reassured about my country's future when I remembered other small- and medium-sized countries which had once occupied that same slot on the U.S. foreign-policy agenda in the second half of the twentieth century: Cuba, Vietnam, Lebanon, Guatemala, El Salvador, Nicaragua, Grenada, and Panama. And Haiti.

In any case, it is clear that the U.S. Administration was eager to help Reynolds and Adams wring from the British such concessions to the nationalist agenda — *aka* the peace process — as would "save the ceasefire," and Clinton's standing as a peacemaker, up to and through the Congressional elections on November 8. In Ireland, these pressures would increase the political prestige and clout of the IRA, and proportionately increase the fury of the unionist population and of the loyalist paramilitaries in particular. This version of a peace process will bring Ireland closer and closer to civil war every day that it continues.

Other terrorist organizations, some of them with designs on the United States itself, will have been studying the tactics through which the IRA has managed to enlist the support of the United States for their program of destabilizing Northern Ireland and disrupting the present United Kingdom. They will note the demonstrated potential of combining blandishments with blackmail. They will note the general vulnerability of democratic governments, in the field of security. And they will note how the word *peace* and the hopes associated with it can be made to serve a terrorist cause. They will note especially the artistry with which a conditional *suspension* of violence can be made to supplement the violence itself and enhance its effectiveness.

The year 1994 is more like Orwell's *Nineteen Eighty-four* than the real 1984 was. In 1994, we are beginning to understand the full force of the Orwellian slogan, "Peace Means War."

The manner in which the United States has been led to dance to a terrorist tune over Ireland is symbolic of certain question marks over the future of democracy. It shows the vulnerability of democracy to terrorist manoeuvres, especially at election times. More generally, it reveals a weakness to which democracies are exposed, in consequence of the desire of their electorates for peace. The desire itself, obviously, is laudable, but it can be exploited for purposes which are the very reverse. Terrorists and other aggressors are well aware that the desire of most people for peace is a resource which they can exploit to their advantage.

The classic example of this is, of course, the policy of appeasement followed by the Western democracies towards Mussolini and then Hitler from 1935 to 1939. This policy became discredited, but it was extremely popular with the British and French press and publics at the time. Baldwin and Chamberlain, Laval and Daladier were responsive to the yearning of their peoples for peace. And the appeasement policy was internationally applauded. Throughout the thirties, Nobel Peace Prizes went to pacifists, mostly British and French pacifists whose activities were consistently — though altogether inadvertently — beneficial to Hitler.

As a result of this prolonged peace process, Hitler got back control over the Rhineland, secured the abolition of all limitations on German rearmament, and acquired Austria and Sudetenland. We now know that if the Western powers had been ready to risk war in 1936, over Hitler's order to his then-tiny army to occupy the demilitarized Rhineland, Hitler would have fallen and war been averted. The peace process, from 1936 on, meant that the West had to fight, three years later, a Germany grown immensely formidable, through the yearning of the West for peace.

It is said that democracies are necessarily peace-loving because ordinary people love peace, whereas arbitrary princes and dictators use war and the threat of war as an instrument of policy. As a historical generalization, this has some flaws. Britain was already a full democracy at the end of the nineteenth century, under the forms of a constitutional monarchy. But the Boer War was immensely popular with the British public at its beginning in 1899, and remained so for most of its course. It was only in retrospect that it turned sour. In 1914, both the British and French democracies were enthusiastic about the war. Among all the belligerents, the socialist parties, hitherto pacifists, were converted into warlike nationalists, by the popular mood, of which they themselves formed part.

It was through the experience of the First World War that the idea of war became repulsive to the democracies. If that experience did not have that effect, then people would have been incapable of learning. Yet the relation of democracy to peace is still problematic. The best way of averting war may be through the running of a limited calculated risk: as over the Rhineland in 1936. But the people at large can never be in a position to make such calculations. To run *any* risk of general war is unpopular. We know now, through records that have come to light, that there was really no risk in maintaining the demilitarization, because the German military would have acquiesced, and dumped the foolhardy Hitler. Even at the time, there was no serious *military* risk. But there was a *political* risk. The ex-Allies could easily have beaten the German army at that time, even if it had chosen to fight. But the political consequences of such a victory could have been ruinous for the Western leaders concerned. They would have seemed — or so they thought — reckless and bloody-minded, making too light of the dangers of a new world war. And so they would have been replaced.

The central problem of democracy in relation to peace may be stated as follows: Democratic process is an endless series of popularity contests. Democratic leaders, selected through such contests, and aiming to be reselected, are thereby conditioned to prize popularity over all other things. They cannot, therefore, subject their popularity, in the present and immediate future, to serious risk, for the sake of long-term benefits to their peoples. They are not conditioned, indeed, to think about the long term at all. The long term is somebody else. The here and now is *me*, and so . . .

This tendency, inbuilt in the nature of democracy, has been accentuated in the late twentieth century by television and by opinion polls which reflect television. A president tends to be governed by his ratings. When the ratings slip, he is impelled to do something that will bring them back up. Whether the something is wise or foolish, whether it is in the long-term interests of his people or not, are irrelevant considerations. All that matters is whether the something is likely to be popular. And if the something turns out to be unpopular, or if it later becomes unpopular, why then of course you drop it and try the reverse until that, in its turn, ceases to be popular. And so on, *ad infinitum* and *ad nauseam*.

You may perhaps think that I am talking about the Clinton Administration. I am, but not *only* his administration. This malady, for such it is, has afflicted every

American president since Eisenhower. In discussing the problems of democracy I am concentrating for the moment on the American presidency because that is by far the most important elective office in the world. And if democracy should fail in the United States — and that is not impossible — democracy would, quite speedily, become unfashionable in the rest of the world.

So let us look briefly at American presidents in the second half of our century in relation to the problems of democracy, both the inbuilt problem and the recent aggravations of that problem.

Dwight Eisenhower was the first president of the United States to be elected in the second half of this century. He was also the last president who, faced with an important decision, did not worry about his popularity rating. When Anthony Eden and Guy Mollet decided, late in 1956, to invade Egypt, in collusion with Israel, they knew that the Eisenhower Administration would not approve of what they were doing. All the same, they calculated that they could get away with it, in November 1956, on the eve of a presidential election. According to their calculations, Eisenhower would not dare to condemn or confront them, because of the importance of the Jewish vote in New York City, Chicago, and Los Angeles. By offending that voting bloc he might lose the great states of New York, Illinois, and California, and along with those the election itself.

The calculators had got it wrong. Eisenhower ignored the electoral implications and came down like a ton of bricks on Israel, Britain, and France. He was hardest of all on Israel, threatening, by implication, to leave it to the mercy of the USSR if it failed to withdraw from Sinai. Israel withdrew from Sinai, Britain and France from the Canal Zone. The Suez episode was over. Eisenhower was re-elected easily.

Wrong in the case of Eisenhower, the same calculators would have been correct in the case of any of his successors. Eisenhower had not been bred to democratic politics. He was not conditioned to ask, before any decision, "Will this be popular or not?" Under military conditions that does not enter into decision-making. If the decisions are right in themselves, and if other factors are propitious, they will result in victory. Victory is the most popular thing on earth, and it was his victory in the Second World War that made Eisenhower president.

I had better be careful at this point, because I sound as if I am making an argument for military rule. Not so. Democracy, despite all its weaknesses, is still the best political system that exists or is likely to exist. Military rule, wherever tried, is miserable by comparison with genuine democracy. (Military rule with a democratic facade, which exists in many countries, is probably worse even than straightforward military rule.) But democracy has its specific weaknesses, through — among other things — the short-term nature of the relentless quest for popularity. Those weaknesses are being accentuated by the conditions of the late twentieth century. That is why it is important to explore these weaknesses as I am doing in relation to certain American presidencies.

I am not saying that a successful soldier necessarily makes a good president. The presidency of Ulysses S. Grant is conclusive evidence to the contrary. My point is that persons bred to the military profession — and certain other professions — are more likely than professional politicians to be able to resist the chronic ailment of democracy: the craving for short-term popularity. The outstanding example in this kind is the first and greatest president of the United States, George Washington. No subsequent president has been as indifferent to popularity. Washington fully backed the unpopular Alexander Hamilton, his secretary of the treasury, in the unpopular enterprise of providing the United States with a sound currency. When war broke out between Britain and revolutionary France, early in 1793, the French cause was overwhelmingly popular with Americans, and the Girondin government made a spirited effort, through its diplomatic and consular representatives in the U.S., to draw the U.S. into war with Britain. The French revolutionary rhetoric about "the common cause of liberty," and about the French Revolution being the continuation and fulfilment of the American one, seemed attractive and convincing to most Americans. In the teeth of all that, Washington, heedless of popularity, proclaimed and enforced American neutrality. That neutrality was the basis of the spectacular growth in American commerce and prosperity in the most crucial years for the young republic: the last years of the eighteenth century and the first years of the nineteenth.

In considering the workings of the popularity factor in democracy, it is instructive to compare the conduct in this period of the "amateur" politician, Washington, and the career politician, Thomas Jefferson. Both as Washington's first secretary of state, and later as a private citizen with a strong political power base in his native Virginia, Jefferson covertly sought to undermine Washington's policies and his authority, targeting Hamilton, whom Jefferson hated, and also Washington's "desertion" of the cause of liberty, incarnate in revolutionary France. Jefferson's opposition to Washington was mostly covert, but not entirely so: just the kind of blend that professional politicians appreciate. Even while he was Washington's secretary of state he was making it known — mainly through James Madison, effectively leader of the opposition in the House of Representatives at the time — that his heart was in the right place, over Hamilton's policies and over the French Revolution. The right place was not Washington's place. But it was the place where popularity lay. The first secretary of state of the first president was already laying the foundations of his own future emergence as the third president of the United States.

Jefferson's courtship of popularity was not short-term but lifelong. But the demands of popularity determined his short-term decisions, as for example on where to stand about Washington's Proclamation of Neutrality. As Washington's secretary of state, Jefferson was responsible for promulgating that proclamation. But he allowed it to be known that he was doing so only out of personal loyalty to the president, and that he had the gravest misgivings about Washington's judgement in this matter, since Jefferson's sympathies were with revolutionary France. His resignation as secretary of state at the end of the year that saw the Proclamation of Neutrality seemed to confirm this view of the matter.

While revolutionary France had become unpopular with Americans generally by the late 1790s, pro-French sentiment, of a rather vague description, re-mained important among the political class in the southern states, Thomas Jefferson's power base. It may seem odd, at first sight, that the class of people in the United States which was most enamoured of the French Revolution was Jefferson's own class: the slave-owning aristocracy of the South. The detestation of the same class for Hamilton's financial policies is easy to explain. All these Southern gentlemen were loaded with debt, and sound finance was simply not in their interests. But one would have thought that the French Revolution, which wiped out the French aris-tocracy, would not have had much appeal for them either. The repercussions of the French Revolution, in Jefferson's own time, destroyed the slave-owning ar-istocracy in San Domingo (now known as Haiti) along with a lot of other people. If *égalité* had come to Vir-ginia, it would have destroyed Jefferson himself and all his friends.

So the enthusiasm of the Southern planters for the French Revolution seems to require some explanation. In my reading about the period, I have not so far found any. So let me hazard a guess. I believe the sources of the appeal of the French Revolution to Jefferson's class consisted mainly of two factors. The first was the popularity of the French Revolution among Americans generally, based on the general feeling that it was a continuation and endorsement of the American Revolution, and faced the same enemy, the British Empire. The second factor was that the general popularity of the French Revolution ran counter to the interests of the class whose power the Southern slave-owners most hated and resented: the class whose ablest and most powerful representative was Thomas Jefferson's hated rival, Alexander Hamilton. The class which Hamilton represented was the moneyed interest in the great seaports of the North. Britain and revolutionary France had been at war since February 1793. Because of British power at sea, an alliance with France would ruin the commerce of the United States, which was mainly in Northern hands. Washington, a Virginian who had become an American, saw that such a development would be ruinous, not merely to a particular class in a particular region, but to the growth and prosperity of America. He therefore issued his Proclamation of Neutrality, knowing it to be unpopular but convinced that it was the right course.

Jefferson never publicly opposed the policy of neutrality. That would have meant confrontation with Washington. Even if Washington were on an unpopular course for the moment, confrontation with the victor of Yorktown was not a tempting option for a rising politician in the 1790s. Jefferson accepted neutrality, while letting it be known that he did so reluctantly and urging that neutrality be interpreted in the sense most favourable to the French, and least favourable to the British. That was where popularity was to be found, and where popularity was, there also was Thomas Jefferson.

Jefferson was the archetype of a *normal* democratic politician: the sort of person who might be expected to rise to the top in a system where success depends on popularity. America has been saved by presidents who were popular but capable of risking their popularity when they believed the national interest to require that. Washington, Lincoln, Franklin Delano Roosevelt were presidents of that stamp. So was Eisenhower, though at a lower level. The rest of the presidents have been more like Jefferson, specialists in the cultivation of popularity.

All of the presidents who have succeeded Eisenhower have been specialists of the same stripe. The only one of them who was not a career politician belonged to the *only* profession that is more popularity-oriented even then democratic politics. I refer to the actor-president, Ronald Reagan.

Of all those latter presidents, the only one who has appeared to shine, in retrospect, is John F. Kennedy. Yet JFK, brilliant as was his political style, was quite a standard popularity-first man. He knew, in 1962-63, that it would be contrary to America's interests to commit additional forces to Vietnam, but he did it anyway, with an eye to winning the presidential election of 1964, which of course he did not live to see.

I wonder whether democracy can survive an unbroken series of specialists of that kind at the top? As we look back, the survival of democracy seems to have depended on'the emergence, at moments of supreme crisis, of leaders capable of risking their popularity: Churchill, Roosevelt. To an uncomfortable degree, therefore, the survival of democracy would appear to be a matter of luck. How long will the luck last? Will it last to the end of the next century? Will it be even a memory by the end of the third millennium? I shall come back to those questions.

The contrast between Washington and Jefferson has something to tell us about the workings of democracy. But the posthumous career of Jefferson has something to tell us about a value system inseparable from democracy: liberalism. And just as the career of the living Jefferson is disturbing in relation to democracy, so is his posthumous career disturbing in relation to liberalism.

In his lifetime, Jefferson was a brilliant manipulator of the media, as befitted a dedicated and successful seeker after popularity. But this popularity seeker and media manipulator was unique in this: his success in those domains has long outlasted his lifetime. He burnished his personal image with such skill in his own day that its lustre has lasted into our own. Jefferson was indeed a political genius. Not the kind that generations of his admirers have delighted to depict. A different kind of genius: more disturbing, but not less interesting. A genius, above all, in the moulding of public opinion.

In the study of posthumous reputations, there is nothing more remarkable than the way in which Jefferson's reputation not merely continued to flourish, but actually grew, in the United States after the Civil War. For Jefferson was pre-eminently a sectional politician, a consistent defender of the interests of the slave-owning South. He favoured anything that could damage or break up the North: war with Britain, Shay's Rebellion in Massachusetts, the Whiskey Rebellion in Western Pennsylvania. He lived to see, in the 1820s, the beginnings of the great controversy that was to lead, gradually but inexorably, to the Civil War. In this controversy he championed the cause of the Southern slave-owners. But he did so in the guise of an *opponent* of slavery. The extension of slavery to every new state in the Union would, he explained, *dilute* slavery and ultimately cause it to disappear. Jefferson's fellow slave-owners were delighted with the ingenuity of this argument but — strangely — it did nothing to diminish their enthusiasm for the extension of slavery.

In theory, Jefferson was a lifelong opponent of the institution of slavery; in practice, he continued to hold slaves. He had recommended manumission, but failed to practise it himself. He was at the same time the most eloquent exponent of the cause of liberty. Liberty for him was a self-evident absolute. His mind was not preoccupied, as was the mind of his contemporary, Edmund Burke, with the problems of reconciling liberty and order. Yet this absolutist libertarian was also a lifelong owner of about one hundred and fifty slaves.

So how can the great lover of liberty deny that paramount boon to so many of his fellow human beings? At this point in Jefferson's discourses on the themes of liberty and slavery — as in his *Notes on Virginia* — we can hear the equivalent of a discreet cough. Human beings. Are blacks human beings? The benevolent philosopher would certainly like to think so, but the rigorous scientist is not sure that the evidence as yet warrants a positive answer to that question. The philosopher in Jefferson would like to think that blacks are equal to whites, in intellectual capacity, but the scientist is not convinced that this is actually so. Through discourse of this kind, the stark contradiction between liberty and slavery is mellowed and mitigated. If those to whom liberty is denied are not really human, then the problem disappears altogether. Jefferson never affirms that they are not human, but he allows the possibility to be glimpsed, with ostensible regret.

I find it troubling that a thinker of this kind should be perhaps the greatest cultural hero of the Western democracies and certainly of the United States. And I find it especially troubling that the author of a few dozen peremptory affirmations about liberty should have become the secular patron saint of modern liberal intellectuals, mostly in America, but also in the wider culture of the English language. The Sage of Monticello is venerated, in the relevant circles, as the greatest source of political wisdom within the Western tradition. Yet if Jefferson was a deep political thinker, he kept his deep political thoughts to himself. He was indeed a person of extraordinary and versatile ingenuity and talent. He was also an extremely astute and successful political operator, cultivating the absentminded and fastidious style of the politician who is so good at his business that he comes to be regarded as above politics. Jefferson was a much more formidable practitioner of the ordinary and not very edifying arts of practical politics than he gave himself out to be, or than his latter-day admirers assume him to have been. But of political wisdom, in the grand sense attributed to him by those admirers, there is not a trace in all the massive tomes of his collected papers.

Much of that mass of paper is not about politics at all but about farming, architecture, travel, and science. Of the political writings, by far the most important is, of course, Jefferson's draft of the Declaration of Independence. The Declaration is, of course, a magnificent manifesto. But it is not the object of a manifesto to convey original political thinking. The object is to stimulate people to a particular course of action by expressing thoughts they already think, while clothing these in language of a solemn and exalted character. The Declaration was necessarily a collective document, but I don't doubt that the final draft, which was not *entirely* Jefferson's, was mainly his. The clothing of popular ideas in exalted language was a Jeffersonian art.

In any case, it has ever since been accepted that Jefferson was, as he claimed in the epitaph he chose for his own tomb, "The Author of the Declaration of Independence." And this is the main source of the veneration which Jefferson has inspired in successive

generations of Americans. His was a consciously secular mind which made a God out of liberty. In the
pantheon of the American civil religion, Jefferson oc-
cupies, for most Americans, the second place after
Washington. For many American intellectuals, he oc-
cupies the first place, for Jefferson was himself an
intellectual, while Washington most definitely was
not. In any case, Jefferson's role was especially holy,
even for most Americans, because of its special close-
ness to the numinous. The Declaration of Independence is the supremely sacred scripture of the
American civil religion. Jefferson's role as the man
who wrote down the scripture is analogous to the role
of the Prophet Muhammad taking down the Blessed
Koran at the dictation of an angel of God.

At this point, I must confess that my discourse is
taking a turn that surprises me. The thrust of my
argument, up to the point where I came to consider the
significance of the Declaration, was to expose the hollowness of the posthumous cult of Jefferson as a sage,
in comparison with the known facts of the career of a
political opportunist. I wished to go on from that to
suggest that this hollowness, at the centre of the Western liberal intellectual tradition, raised questions
about the durability of that tradition. But then, in the
context of the Declaration, I began to see something
else: that the cult of Jefferson, incongruous though it
may seem in comparison with the facts of his political
career, may actually be a bonding factor in American
life, and a factor making for strength and continuity in
the American political system.

On the one hand, Jefferson is the Sage of Monticello, a characteristic Enlightenment thinker of the late eighteenth century. On the other hand, he is the prophet who wrote down the sacred scripture of America at the bidding of that most exalted of archangels whose task it is to expound God's providential designs for His Chosen People, the Americans.

The effect of the cult of Jefferson, therefore, is to invest the secular and ostensibly wholly rational Enlightenment with an aura of revelation and the numinous.

This is certainly a most paradoxical development. If it were consciously analysed, it would give scandal both to religious people and to rationalists. But it is not analysed: it is a matter of culturally transmitted assumptions and habits. There is a rich irony here. Jefferson in his lifetime was a bitter ideological enemy of Edmund Burke, from the time of the publication of Burke's *Reflections on the Revolution in France* in November 1790. Yet the posthumous *cult* of Jefferson, as transmitted from generation to generation in the culture, through inherited assumptions and habits, is a Burkean phenomenon and not a Jeffersonian one, and all the better for that.

Enlightenment ideas are far more solidly established in America than anywhere else, because there, as nowhere else, they are firmly embedded in the massive edifice of sacral nationalism. Putting it another way, the American Enlightenment resists decay because it is pickled in holy brine.

That sounds funny and is a bit. Most people's religions and most people's nationalisms do look a bit funny to those who were not brought up in them. To me, a student of America who is not American, and a student of religion who is not religious, at least in any formal sense, the American civil religion certainly has its diverting side, as well as its impressive side, and the two sides may be more dependent on one another than we are in the habit of noticing.

One of the least known, but not the least significant, manifestations of the American civil religion is an institution known as the National Prayer Breakfast. Prayer breakfasts, as a spontaneous manifestation of community religious life, are quite old. Among American Catholics they take the form of the Holy Name Society's Communion Breakfasts, attendance at which is practically mandatory for members of the New York City police department. Prayer breakfasts have long played an important part in the religious and communal life of rural and small-town Protestant America. But the *National* Prayer Breakfast is fairly new. It was instituted by President Eisenhower in 1953, the first year of his first term. In its origin it is a product of the Cold War and also of American party politics. In relation to the Cold War, it made a large, relevant and comforting point: God had to be on the side of the United States against godless Communism. In American party politics it made a very sharp point indeed, against the Democrats. The implication was that God was back in Washington, after twenty years of Democratic rule under Roosevelt and Truman. Under the Democrats, Washington had been infiltrated by the agents of atheistic Communism, facilitated by liberal and secular elements, high in the councils of the Democratic Party.

The creation of the National Prayer Breakfast sent a clear signal both to religious America and to official America that all that was over. The American nation was a prayerful nation. There was something un-American about a refusal to pray. Senator Joe McCarthy, during this period, was directing his main attacks on the liberal and secular elements in American society, as prime security risks. His most famous smear — "Adlai, I mean Alger" — was a calculated slip of the tongue, confusing the respected liberal Adlai Stevenson with the convicted perjurer Alger Hiss. In its inception and in its intention, then, the creation of the National Prayer Breakfast was a Counter-Enlightenment move. A series of further moves of that type could have taken the Enlightenment right out of its special sphere in the American civil religion.

That didn't happen, nor, I think, did anyone ever seriously intend that it should. The Republicans who set up the breakfast saw it as a blunt instrument for preventing a Democratic comeback rather than as a move in a profound philosophical-ideological agenda. But even as a weapon against the Democrats, the identification of godliness with American nationalism proved two-edged. Joe McCarthy was a Catholic and a Republican. But it was his combination of Catholicism and Republicanism that made possible the election of a Catholic Democrat — John F. Kennedy — to succeed Eisenhower in 1960.

Let me explain that one. It had been generally assumed,

until the 1950s, that a Catholic could not be elected president of the United States. The received wisdom was that whereas the big cities could vote for a Catholic, rural and small-town America, especially in the South, never would. Joe McCarthy changed all that by demonstrating that a Roman Catholic could be the toughest anti-Communist in the business. Specifically, by targeting leading figures in the Eastern establishment as soft on Communism, McCarthy won the hearts of poor rural Protestants who knew that McCarthy's targets looked down on them, quite as much as on Catholics, if not more. The general anti-Communist fever of the period made Catholics upwardly mobile, politically. For the Bible Belt, by 1960, Antichrist was as menacing as ever, but he had shifted his address from the Vatican, Rome, to the Kremlin, Moscow. The way was open — though only just so — for the election of John F. Kennedy to the presidency.

Kennedy continued the National Prayer Breakfast as have all subsequent presidents, so that it has long since lost its original party-political edge, and along with that its Counter-Enlightenment emphasis. It is now primarily a celebration of American nationalism, and as such can share the American civil religion quite comfortably with the American branch of the Enlightenment, which descends of course from the English and Scottish branches of that movement and is therefore vaguely reverential towards religion-in-general, rather than contemptuously hostile towards all religions, like the French *lumière*.

In January of 1989, in the second half of the second

term of Ronald Reagan's presidency, I received an invitation to attend the National Prayer Breakfast in the International Ballroom of the Washington Hilton. There were about 5,000 people gathered on the floor of the ballroom. Most of them seemed to be young male evangelical Protestants from small-town America: young and upwardly mobile, even right now and here below for the moment.

On a dais of marked elevation were leading representatives of the whole American national establishment: the prayer breakfast committees of both Houses of Congress, including the speakers of both Houses; justices of the Supreme Court; the then-chairman of the Joint Chiefs of Staff; the governors or deputy governors of all the states of the union, and the mayors of all the major cities. At precisely eight a.m. President Reagan and the First Lady entered and took their places at the table. When the splendid gathering on the dais and the humbly prayerful on the ballroom floor had all taken their seats, the chairman of the prayer breakfast committee, Congressman Ralph Regula of Ohio, who was that year also chairman of the prayer breakfast committee of the House of Representatives, rose to deliver the opening prayer. It was a short one, and I wrote it down in full:

"Oh, Lord! Help us, in the excitement of the presence here amongst us this morning of the president of the United States, to remember also the presence of Your Son, Jesus Christ. Amen."

I looked around me at the bright, clear evangelical faces but did not see in any the slightest gleam of any sense of the incongruous. Rather, the sense of the combined presence of Jesus Christ and Ronald Reagan seemed to be the very heart of the national and supernatural mystery being celebrated in the International Ballroom of the Hilton Hotel in Washington, D.C.

I thought that National Prayer Breakfast and especially that opening prayer very funny at the time. But things that are funny can also have a serious aspect. Turning these matters over in my mind in retrospect, I wondered what would happen if American institutions could be entirely divested of that numinous dimension which the American civil religion confers on them. The American Constitution is the greatest institutional repository and transmitter of Enlightenment values, not merely in America, but in the Western world, permeated by American values. What if the nimbus of awe which has so long surrounded the Constitution should fade into the light of common day? What if the nimbus should then light on a form of American nationalism that would be aware of nothing above itself?

God moves in a mysterious way and so, it seems, does the Enlightenment. Old Voltairian though I am, I can *almost* murmur "Amen" to Congressman Regula's opening prayer.

III
THINGS FALL APART

IN THE FIRST CHAPTER, I opened with W. B. Yeats's "The Second Coming." I should think that the lines from that poem most relevant to our own time are the famous and often-quoted ones:

Things fall apart; the centre cannot hold;
Mere anarchy is loosed upon the world . . .

In some ways these lines may seem more appropriate to our own time than they were to the world about which Yeats was writing, more than seventy years ago, in the aftermath of the First World War. We have seen the Soviet Union falling apart and Yugoslavia and Czechoslovakia and then some of the pieces of those former polities themselves disintegrating and many signs of disintegration elsewhere in the world. We may be, perhaps, thinking of disintegration as the dominant characteristic of our world, and likely to extend indefinitely into the next millennium. This would probably be a mistake.

Let me add that, despite recent election results, I

would not include Canada in the number of disintegrating polities. But I would advise thoughtful Québécois, pondering a future referendum option, to visit Bratislava and hear the second thoughts of many Slovaks who formerly supported the decision to break up Czechoslovakia and set up an independent Slovakia. At present, the new Czech Republic is doing rather well, while Slovakia, on the whole, is not. Breaking up things is not always a good idea, although it has seemed so to millions of people on this eve of the millennium. The noise of things falling apart is all around us, but that is nothing new.

The world has been falling apart for a very long time, if that reflection can be of any consolation to us in the late twentieth century.

The poet Horace wrote about the phenomenon, a little more than two thousand years ago. According to him, if the world were to fall apart, the ruins would leave the man who was just and tenacious of purpose in a dauntless condition. *Impavidum ferient ruinae.*

To be fair to the poet Horace, he was not engaging in any personal heroics. He never affected to be especially just or tenacious of purpose. He acknowledged that he had run away from the Battle of Philippi, leaving his little shield behind him. *Non bene*: Not very creditably. Horace was an honest man, except when he was writing for a governmental commission and to governmental stipulation. The ode about the world falling apart — *Si fractus illabatur orbis* — was official business: a state ode. The man who was just and tenacious of purpose was not the poet, or a model either for poets or ordinary mortals, but Caesar Augustus, the top politician of the age. Augustus had actually experienced the world coming apart: the terrible terminal convulsions of the Roman republic, the assassination of Julius Caesar, and then the division of the Roman heritage into an Eastern and a Western empire. Fragments of all those ruins had struck Augustus but had not daunted him. More than that, Augustus personally had restored the shattered world. He now presided over a united Roman empire, embracing the whole of the Mediterranean world. What history had deconstructed had been reconstructed by the will and skill of a true Roman hero.

That at least was the picture which Horace and his fellow eulogists sought to present. There was, no doubt, too much in it of what a later age would call "the cult of the personality" — although the Augustan eulogists had better material to work on than most of their successors, at divers courts and under divers administrations over the next two thousand years.

There are two points about the Augustan example that should, I believe, be of abiding interest to us. The first is that worlds that fall apart can come together again. It is true also that the world that comes together can fall apart yet again, as happened to the Roman Empire under the successors of Augustus. Yet that empire, though politically extinct, lived on in the culture of all its successor states. The Judaeo-Hellenic culture which had permeated the empire — and helped to dissolve it — was transmitted fruitfully to the successor states. And the successors came to include nations — like the United States and Canada and Australia — whose very territorial basis of existence was entirely unknown to the contemporaries of Augustus.

When a world falls apart, that is not necessarily the end of the world.

Horace was writing near the beginning of what we call the Christian Era. He didn't know about the possibility of a Christian Era, but he was very conscious of living at the beginning of *some* kind of new era. He personally was not a religious man. He was a child of the Hellenistic Enlightenment. He spoke of himself as *parcus deorum cultor et infrequens*, a stingy and infrequent worshipper of the gods. Yet he and Virgil were the priests of a new religion, that of the divinized Roman emperor. The function of these poet-priests was to stop the world from falling apart by consolidating it around a universal cult, which proposed to co-opt every other cult. That effort failed, partly because of the refusal, first of the Jews and then of the Christians, to be co-opted to the cult. But it remains of interest to us, because something like it is among the millennial possibility of the human future. For nineteenth-century writers, world government was a benign dream. For writers of twentieth-century dystopias — like David Karp's *One* — it has been a nightmare. Either way, the possibility is there.

I began with a poet contemplating the notion (and recent reality) of a world falling apart, the better to glorify the achievement of a world brought together. In what follows, I want to discuss the role of poetry, in its widest sense — including drama and opera — in relation to politics in its widest sense: the fallings apart and comings together of worlds.

I don't know that poetry would be thought of today by most people as being among the performing arts. Yet historically it has been perhaps the most basic and the most powerful of these. It has been felt to possess quasi-magical faculties of exaltation and degradation. It was meant to be *performed*, that is to say spoken aloud, declaimed in ceremonies of state, as were Horace's state odes and the prophetic passages in Virgil. In short, poetry had from of old, and has retained into modern times, certain political functions.

From very ancient times, the poet had been a praise-singer, a celebrator of ancestors, heroes, chiefs, and dynasties. Poetry was associated with acting out, with song and dance and ritual celebration. Epic poetry was the source and stuff out of which drama was made. All this was part of a living process of holding the world together: a familiar established world, home to the poets whom it nourished and who nourished it. But poetry could also anathematize, delegitimize, help to shatter worlds. In celebrating Rome it could call down fire on Alexandria and vice versa of course. One might say: Who remembers the vice versa, the poetry of the losers? None of that entered the classical canon directly, but something of it can still be heard in the doom-laden melancholy of certain passages of Virgil which some have traced to the poet's Celtic roots. The poetry of defeated peoples has probably played a significant part in the break-up of empires, the falling apart of worlds. The Aeneid springs from the defeat of Troy.

Is politics among the performing arts? I believe it always has been, in some of its aspects, and that the importance of these aspects is now increasing with the increasing dominance of television. We can hardly forget, in this context, that a professional movie actor recently played the part of president of the United States in the White House itself, for a run of two full terms.

On stage, Ronald Reagan made like a superb president of the United States. Off stage, he seems to have spent most of his time either asleep or reminiscing about old movies. But that didn't worry his audience, so long as his performance on stage was giving satisfaction. Who cares how an actor spends his time when he is resting? Some of the non-histrionic aspects of the presidency got a bit neglected during this period. There was that budget deficit, for example, but that was something for Reagan's successors to worry about.

Reagan was always master of his script and judged the merits of the script solely by audience response. When he found the audience tiring of the old script, as he did by halfway through the second term of his show, he got himself a new script, dropping the evil empire stuff, since it no longer played, and providing himself with a new role as peacemaker extraordinary. The new role happened to coincide with the beginning of the collapse of the Soviet Union, and Reagan improvised a finale in which he played the part of the man who had planned it all.

The fusion of showbiz and politics has never been

as thoroughly exemplified as by the Reagan presidency, but *some* element of showbiz is inseparable from all politics, not least from the American presidency. Showbiz politics can be competent or the reverse. George Bush was as deficient in histrionic skills and intuition as Reagan was proficient in the same. And that deficiency in Bush was largely responsible for his failure to win a second term. Dramatically speaking, the highlight of the Bush presidency was the Republican Convention of 1992, at Houston, Texas, in the run-up to the presidential election. And that show was a turkey. Like all party conventions in the late twentieth century, this one was planned as you would plan a theatrical showpiece, but for a political purpose. It was aimed at the television audience, in the hope that its impact would swing the November elections to the Republicans.

The only trouble was that the performance was poorly planned and executed. The theme of that disastrous political production was "Family Values," which was wrongly felt to be surefire stuff. This theme needs to be handled gently and with sensitivity. At that convention a crude version of the subject was blared out with an odious camera-drunk exhibitionism that put off even people who were basically on their side, while outraging those who were not. Also, convention planners forgot, relative to the issue of abortion, that while "pro-life" people are a lot noisier as a lobby, "pro-choice" people are much more numerous, especially among women. The Houston Convention tilted the women's vote quite heavily against the Republican ticket and left the Democrats in control both of the presidency and of both Houses of Congress. Republican politicians running for election or re-election in 1994's mid-term Congressional elections turned pale at the very mention of family values and shamelessly deserted pro-life for pro-choice.

Good showbiz can have a strong influence on democratic politics, as witness FDR's fireside chats and Kennedy's Camelot. But I know of no bit of good political showbiz in this decade that has had as much influence over democratic process and policy making as has been exerted by the miserably *poor* showbiz of that Houston Convention.

Let me now return from those modern instances to the vaster theme of the performing arts in history. It is not possible to say with certainty whether the results of the performing arts aspect of social and political history have been on balance benign or malign. I opt personally for benign, as I shall show in my conclusion, but I confess this is an act of faith rather than the result of analysis. Such matters may well be beyond the range of human computation. In any case, those of us who claim that in general the role of the performing arts — in the widest sense — has been benign have quite a lot to explain away. Over long periods of time, the favoured and sanctioned forms of spectacle have been bloody and cruel. Human sacrifice has been a performing art in many cultures. The devouring of living human beings by wild beasts was the spectacle that played to packed audiences in the Coliseum under the patronage of the later Roman emperors.

Later forms of cruel spectacle were more didactic in intent. There was the Spanish Inquisition with its acts of faith: *autos da fé*, the public burnings of Jews and heretics for the salvation of souls and the edification of the faithful. In the Protestant culture, trials and burnings of witches appeared to satisfy similar needs. Nor did the Enlightenment bring an end to all the bloody charades, though it did discourage the explicitly religious varieties. In 1793, the show trials of the king and queen of France, followed by their public execution, constituted the central ritual of the transition from monarchy to republic, a ritual transition brilliantly explored by Professor Susan Dunn in her magisterial work *The Deaths of Louis XVI* (Princeton, 1994). Human sacrifice had returned, but this time to the accompaniment of the rhetoric of the Enlightenment. And it returned again in our own century with rhetoric and practices imitated from French revolutionary sources, in Stalin's show trials and Stalin's terror.

Yet it can reasonably be argued that the general tendency, in the West at least, has been towards gentler forms of theatre and ritual. Very early within Judaism, human sacrifice was outlawed, a transition reflected in the story of Abraham and Isaac. In later Judaism and in Christianity the sacrifice became purely symbolic. As for the Coliseum, its excesses aroused such general disgust as to discredit the late-Roman culture from which it came — rather like the Houston Convention if on a larger scale. Things like the Spanish Inquisition and witch-hunting are now universally repudiated by all the Christian churches. The admirers of the

French Revolution generally repudiate the terror as an aberration. Stalin's terror was repudiated by the Communists themselves, even before Soviet Communism itself collapsed.

So we may reasonably feel that, given a chance, human beings have a tendency to behave better, and to devise more refined forms of spectacle, theatre, and ritual. With this trend of thought, certain lines of Shakespeare come almost automatically to mind:

> Blood hath been shed ere now, i' the olden time,
> Ere humane statute purged the gentle weal . . .

Yet the words carry a warning within them from their dramatic source. Shakespeare, with cosmic irony, puts those benevolent-sounding words into the mouth of a serial murderer — a Scottish serial murderer whose very name is to this very day unmentionable in theatrical circles.

By a cruel paradox, it was much easier a hundred years ago than it is now to have a firm faith in the benevolent power of progress. In between we have had the two world wars, Gulag, the Holocaust. After all that, faith in progress remains possible, but it has necessarily grown more tentative and more humble.

I should like at this point to consider the relationship of the performing arts, and of one performing art in particular, to the life and career of Adolf Hitler. This is quite a disturbing relationship, but one that is instructive. To see how it works, we need to look at it in a little detail.

During the Cold War and as a result of its necessities it became extremely fashionable to see the Nazi period as a unique aberration. Aberration is often a comforting concept, historiographically. We have seen its usefulness already for admirers of the French Revolution, and for late-twentieth-century Communists in retrospectively coping with the Stalin era. In reality, the terror was not an aberration but inherent in the revolutionary process from the beginning, as Edmund Burke had predicted two years before the terror began. As for Stalin, he was Lenin's partner and heir, and not an aberration from him.

And the Nazi phenomenon was not exactly an aberration either, but a product of the culture of nineteenth-century Europe.

It is true that it was a product that would not have taken the special and sinister form it did without the tremendous pressures of the First World War, and specifically of Imperial Germany's defeat in that war. It was a product, that is to say, both of the Europe to which Imperial Germany had been central and of the falling apart of that world in 1918.

A common Western stereotype of the Cold War period represented Adolf Hitler retrospectively as a semiliterate roughneck devoid of culture. This is a dangerous trivialization. We underestimate Hitler's baleful power if we fail to see that he was a highly intelligent, self-educated person growing up in a highly civilized environment, in an age of mass diffusion of culture. He was familiar with the ideas of Friedrich Nietzsche, and especially with those aspects of Nietzsche's ideas which the academic exponents of "gentle Nietzscheanism" in the Cold War period were to seek to explain out of existence. I shall come back to that in my concluding chapter. At this point it is Hitler's relation to Wagner that I wish to consider. Hitler was a lover of opera; not an ignorant dabbler but a real devotee.

Wagner's operas, and the *Ring Cycle* in particular, play a crucial role in the transition from Imperial to Nazi Germany, and specifically in the career of Hitler. It was a Wagnerian image that supplied the leitmotif of the opening phase of Hitler's political career, in 1919. The image was that of the *Dolchstoss*, the stab in the back that brought down the hero Siegfried in *The Ring*. It was not Hitler who had been responsible for the politicization of that Wagnerian image; that had been the work of the military oligarchs who had ruled Germany in wartime in the name of the Kaiser. After the failure of the last great German offensive in the spring of 1918, the warlords knew that the war was lost but they refused to accept the blame for the defeat. They took refuge in denial, and Wagner came to their aid.

According to the Wagnerian myth of the *Dolchstoss*, Germany had not been defeated at all. She had been stabbed in the back just like Siegfried. Heroic Germany was the victim of treacherous beings of an inferior order: Communists and Jews. That theme was popularized even before the defeat: during the summer and autumn of 1918. But after the war, with Germany facing a revolutionary threat, the theme of the *Dolchstoss* was even more immediately relevant than before. The generals commanding the reduced armed forces that were left to Germany by the Treaty of Versailles hired agitators to spread the word of the *Dolchstoss*, especially among the working class. One of these Wagnerian agitators was Hitler.

In the immediate aftermath of the war, Hitler had been content as it were to whistle his Wagnerian tune, at the bidding of others and for their benefit. But by 1923, he was beginning to have political ideas of his own. The concept of the *Dolchstoss* was always personally congenial to him, even when he was paid to spread it, and it was fundamental, in a different form, to his new plans in the new phase. The leadership of post-Versailles Germany, in the Weimar Republic, including Hitler's former employers, were to be exposed as accessories after the fact in the murder of Siegfried. Hitler would expose them by organizing a revolt against the *Diktat* of Versailles. By crushing that revolt, the Weimar Republic and its military establishment would demonstrate their continuing complicity in the *Dolchstoss*. Hitler, in contrast, would appear as Siegfried *redivivus*. This was the train of thought that led to the political event known in history as the Bierkeller Putsch of 1923 in Munich.

In the case of Hitler, the phrase "the cult of Wagner" is not a mere figure of speech. This was a cult in which he believed as fanatically as any devotee has ever believed in supernatural revelation. The depth of his commitment to the cult is apparent from what he did early in 1923 on the eve of the most important decision of his life to date: that of whether or not to head a rebellion against Versailles, in Munich. In preparation for that decision the daimonic devotee repaired to the great shrine of his faith, at Bayreuth, in Northern Bavaria. There he consulted the oracles, custodians of the shrine, Winifred Wagner and Houston Stewart Chamberlain. Winifred was the composer's daughter-in-law; Chamberlain, the great English apologist for Imperial Germany. Both were passionate German nationalists; Chamberlain had been one of the first proponents, in the service of the generals, of the myth of the *Dolchstoss*, in the closing months of the First World War. Both warmly encouraged the project Hitler was considering. Hitler returned from Bayreuth with his mind made up.

The Bierkeller Putsch of 1923 has been trivialized in retrospect, like so much in Hitler's career. It has been depicted as a ludicrous failure. This is to misunderstand its nature. It was never intended as a serious revolt in the literal and military sense. It was a *symbolic* revolt, resembling, to that extent, and in that respect, the Easter Rising seven years before in Dublin, Ireland; indeed it resembled that earlier and remote revolt also in being closely linked to poetic drama. The Wagner of Dublin's Easter Rising was W. B. Yeats. His intensely nationalist play *Cathleen ni Houlihan*, performed in 1902 with Maud Gonne in the title role, had been an inspiration for the generation of the rebels of 1916. This was a thought that troubled Yeats on his deathbed when he wrote:

Did that play of mine send out
Certain men the English shot?

It probably did. In any case, both revolts were symbolic and sacrificial ritual acts. As in the case of that earlier revolt, the repression of the one in Munich was expected and, in a sense, desired. The repression would recoil against its perpetrators and bring eternal fame to the defeated rebels. In Munich, Hitler acted out a variant on the theme of the *Dolchstoss*, spreading wider the web of guilt to envelop not only Jews and Communists, but the entire Weimar establishment seen as accomplices of Jews and Communists.

On the eve of the 1923 Putsch, Hitler was hardly known in Germany outside limited circles in Bavaria. By the time he was released from prison for his part in the Putsch he was a national figure and a hero of the large *Volkisch* component of German society. Less than ten years more of growing notoriety would bring him to absolute power. And after his release from jail, as on the eve of the act that had taken him there, Hitler went to Bayreuth, this time to receive the congratulations of the custodians of the national and operatic shrine that linked the old Imperial with the nascent National-Socialist Germany.

Hitler's Wagnerianism was no passing phase, but a main inspiration for his frightful vision and apocalyptic mission. In Wagner and Nietzsche — antagonistic though the two men became during their lifetimes — Hitler found a theme that was common, and to his purpose: the theme of higher forms of human life being dragged down and choked by lower forms. Hitler's remedy was one of ghastly simplicity: to exterminate what he regarded as the lower forms. The

Holocaust was to prepare the way for the resurrection of Siegfried and the advent of the Superman.

This was, consciously, a millenarian vision; Hitler, the great propagandist, knew what he was doing when he announced his Thousand Year Reich. He understood the magical resonances that adhere to the idea of a Thousand Years: the heady echoes of the *Book of Revelation* which linger even in consciously secular minds.

I have dwelt on the Wagner-Hitler connection because it is one of the most remarkable, one of the best documented, and at the same time one of the least-known examples of the interaction of art with political history. It also, obviously, represents the ultimate in destructive malignity. It is the most chilling passage in European cultural and social history. I stress the *European*. Wagner and Nietzsche form a major part of our common Europe-rooted culture: the Nazi movement grew out of European history just as the French Revolution did. I have no more thought of blaming contemporary Germans for Nazism than of blaming contemporary Frenchmen for the excesses of the French Revolution.

The arts, like the rest of what Burke calls "our most mysterious nature," have inescapably their malign aspects. Let us now look at some of their benign potentialities, though even these are not lacking in ambiguities.

First, however, I should like to make some distinctions in the matters of worlds falling apart and coming together again. That a world should fall apart is not necessarily a malign phenomenon, nor is its coming together necessarily a benign one. Also our ideas as to whether the world is falling apart or coming together have fluctuated with remarkable velocity, even in the course to date of our present decade. At the beginning of the decade it was being influentially asserted that the world was coming together at such a rate that Western values, such as democracy, capitalism, the rule of law, and freedom of expression would soon be universally accepted and history would have come to an end. Then, by about 1992, it began to be noticed that Francis Fukuyama's confident diagnosis of the end of history in his book *The End of History and the Last Man* hardly seemed to fit the actual conditions prevailing in places like the former Yugoslavia and the former Soviet Union. The idea of coming together ceased to be fashionable and that of falling apart came to enjoy a new vogue. It was at this point those lines of Yeats, from "The Second Coming," began to be quoted with some frequency.

Certainly Yeats's insights are infinitely more profound than poor Mr. Fukuyama's. Yet even Yeats's powers of prescience should not be exaggerated. Anarchy was widespread in 1919, and Yeats's forebodings of a horrible future were fully justified. Yet what was coming, horrible though it was, did not exactly take the form he feared. It was *not* "mere anarchy" that was loosed upon the world between the wars, it was centralized tyranny in the shape of the two most oppressive state-systems the world has ever known: Hitler's Germany and Stalin's Russia. Those were what came

together out of the period of anarchy and in response
to it. And it would be prudent to allow for the possibility that what may now be coming together in the
former Soviet Union may not be much more attractive
than either of the two sets of conditions that preceded
it: the centralized oppression and the anarchy. As A. E.
Housman wrote:

> The troubles of our proud and angry dust
> Are from eternity, and shall not fail.

The Housman doctrine cannot be proved but has yet
to be refuted. History contains an impressive accumu-
lation of evidence in its support; but history, as we
know, covers only a tiny span of the collective experience of the human race. The arts themselves, including
the forms of dance and song and ritual, are certainly
much older than history, and human life on earth is
certainly a success story, if of a disconcerting kind, as
is virtually everything about us. Our species, whatever
its defects, has been exceedingly good at survival even
to the extent that the very abundance of our survival
now threatens the planet we have been crassly exploiting since the opening of the industrial period.

In that matter, the Cairo Conference on Population
and Development, in September 1994, represented a
benign shift in direction. President Clinton, represented at Cairo by Vice-President Al Gore, reversed the
position of his two predecessors and threw the vast
international influence of the United States in favour
of the promotion of contraception and safe abortion.

Bereft of the U.S. support, Vatican opposition was easily swept aside. There is now, for the first time, a sense of purpose in the international community towards checking the ruinous growth in population which represents — to take only one example — the greatest threat to the future of the new South Africa, along with most of the Third World.

Hugely welcome though this shift is, it comes terribly late in the day. Even with the best will in the world, and the most effective action, the malign effects of the population explosion will still be growing throughout the first half of the next century. I shall have more to say about that in my last chapter. Yet, belated though the change is, Cairo still represents a great turning point in human history.

In this benign shift in attitudes to population, the arts in their wider sense have played a major though paradoxical part. They did so through the ironic effects of a tremendous flop: that Republican Convention of 1992 in Houston. That showbiz failure accomplished exactly the opposite of what its planners intended. The devout — or rather the more Enlightened of their number — may see in all this the hand of a greater stage manager in the sky. The rest of us would like to think they are right.

I mentioned rituals that are older than history: rituals of conflict-avoidance, mediation, and conciliation, for example, that may well have played a significant part, over many ages, in the survival of our species. Traces of some of these have lingered into our own time. There is, for example, the sacred mediator known as the "leopard-skin priest" whose procedures have been analysed by the South African anthropologist, David Brokensha. There are the Ogboni men of Western Nigeria whose specialty is the management, by appeasement, of witches: a more civilized method than that practised by the Puritans of New England in the seventeenth century. And in Australia the Cambridge anthropologist, Nicholas Paterson, has described the extremely complex fire ceremony known as *Buluwandi*, practised by the Walbiri people of Central Australia and directed towards the harmless release of hostile tendencies, the working out of tensions, by acting them out.

In modern international life, the United Nations serves similar purposes. More than twenty years ago I wrote a book about the United Nations in its "performing arts" aspect. The book is called *United Nations: Sacred Drama*. The UN is seen as a theatre in which people improvise versions of contemporary history, posture before the world, let off steam, and occasionally devise rituals that can save the peace, most often through saving the faces of powerful people.

Some people are understandably impatient with this approach to the study of the UN. They want it to impose a general peace and, since it has never been in the least equipped to do anything of the kind, they complain about its failure. This is to miss the point. One of the most useful things about the United Nations is its well-demonstrated capacity to be seen to fail.

The classic case in this genre is President

Eisenhower's handling of the Hungarian crisis in 1956. He and Dulles had been calling on the Eastern Europeans to revolt, and implying that the United States would come to their aid if they did. Then the Hungarians actually did revolt. Eisenhower decided not to come to the aid of the rebels, since that would risk world war; a practical calculation, if a belated one. But Eisenhower could not explicitly acknowledge that he was abandoning the Hungarians. This is where the United Nations came in. Eisenhower took the case to the United Nations; the theatre of the General Assembly was filled with the rituals of condemnation while, offstage, the revolt was being crushed.

The United Nations can provide nothing on its own except blessings and curses. If the United States had decided to intervene in Hungary, the United Nations would have blessed that enterprise as it had done in the case of Korea and was to do again over Desert Storm. As the U.S. was not intervening in Hungary, there was no enterprise to bless, and all the United Nations could provide was curses, against the Soviet Union. U.S. officials acknowledged the propriety of the curses but deplored what they described as "the failure of the United Nations to halt the Soviet aggression." The media, on the whole, gratefully followed that lead. They usually do, in such cases.

In short, the Hungarians were ditched, world war was avoided, and the United Nations took all the blame for the ignominious passivity through which the Eisenhower Administration had avoided war.

That was a long time ago, but similar uses of the UN

are still being made today, though more fuzzily. Take
the case of Bosnia and President Clinton. Clinton has
been under pressure to intervene in Bosnia, but he
doesn't want to do so, for adequate reasons. He is
caught between actual and potential televised images.
The images of the horrors of civil war in Bosnia, which
Americans have been seeing on the screen, generate
pressures for American military intervention. But the
president knows that if American forces were actually
sent there, the *new* images on the screens, of dead
American soldiers, would generate pressure for the
recall of the troops. That is not speculation: the
president's memory of what happened in Somalia is
still fresh. So he temporizes, providing the occasional
airstrike with mixed results. He then wonders aloud
why *the United Nations* is not being more effective in
dealing with the problem.

Spectacles of this kind are far from glorious or heart-
warming, but they do have one precious feature. They
represent — as do the older rituals — *a method for the
avoidance of making things even worse than they already
are.* The pressure to make things even worse is rising
in the late twentieth century, with the growing importance of television. The instant harrowing images, im-
pinging on minds with little or no sense of the
significance of their context, are generating such pressures as never before. In these conditions, the rituals of
avoidance, odd and even sordid though they may
appear, are all probably becoming even more needful
for our survival — when that is indeed their object —
than they have been in the past.

Yet a warning note needs to be struck here. The odder and more sordid the rituals of avoidance become, the greater the risk that they will boggle the minds, both of those who devise them and those who accept them, thus endangering the whole heritage of the Enlightenment. These dangers seem to me to be growing on the eve of the millennium, with the growing ascendancy and increasing impudence of the spin-doctors, the shamans of our communications culture.

I am thinking here in particular of the most recent masterpiece of avoidance-ritual: the black political force brazenly designated "Operation Restore Democracy in Haiti." Much can be forgiven to the moral and intellectual demerits of an avoidance-ritual in which the outcome to be avoided is world war. But no such excuse is available over Operation Restore Democracy. Haiti posed no threat of world war. Yet Operation Restore Democracy was an avoidance-ritual, with a precise purpose. What it was immediately designed to avoid was the defeat of Democratic candidates in the November 1994 mid-term Congressional elections. The secondary but all-important thing which it was supposed to avoid was loss of presidential authority over Congress, through the results of those elections and then, in consequence of that lack of authority, failure on Clinton's part to win a second term.

Haiti posed no threat of war. But the arrival of Haitian boat people in Florida threatened to divert votes from Democratic candidates. So also, though in quite a different way, did the later interception of the boat people and their forcible repatriation. So it was necessary to intervene in Haiti to dry up the supply of boat people and eliminate the double threat to the Democratic campaign. But the same logic — entirely premised on the Democratic campaign — required that the object of the intervention be presented in such a light as to serve that campaign. That meant that the object had to be made to appear morally impeccable. With these co-ordinates in mind, the spin doctors came up with one of their most brilliant concoctions, Operation Restore Democracy.

In my concluding chapter I shall be looking again at this operation, this time as an example of degenerative processes affecting the intellect: processes which, if they continue to develop as they are now doing on the eve of the third millennium, may well destroy our Western civilization by around the third century of that millennium.

But here I am concerned with the arts — which always include an element of fiction — and in particular with that application of art to politics which takes the form of avoidance-ritual. And here we have another example of the ethical ambiguity of art. We can distinguish between legitimate forms of avoidance-ritual — where the thing to be avoided is a genuine human disaster — and illegitimate forms, where the thing to be avoided is the defeat of candidates belonging to a particular party in a particular election. But the processes which produce the avoidance-rituals and cause them to be credible take little stock of what anyone may hold to be legitimate or illegitimate.

Man's nature is flawed. And as Edmund Burke said: "Art is man's nature."

In any case, there is a side of art-in-politics, specifically avoidance-ritual, which is conducive to human survival, in certain circumstances. There is also another side, specifically threatening to Western civilization. I shall come back to that side, in my last chapter. But in conclusion here, let me contemplate briefly what I may call the legitimate theatre of survival-oriented avoidance-ritual.

Avoidance, limitation, containment: keys to survival.

Avoidance of making things worse, as they would be made through imprudent military interventions. Limitation: Avoidance of excess, including excess of population (and indeed excess of avoidance-ritual). Containment, as far as possible, of the destructive forces within our psyche. *Containment*, not the Utopian project for the elimination of those forces: a project whose pursuit in practice has carried whole peoples from Gulag to Gulag.

These rather negative-sounding capabilities are the side of the performing arts, in the wider sense, whose acting out is conducive to the avoidance of international conflict. But these negative capabilities are also inherent in the highest levels of the performing arts, in their narrower and often more exalted sense. Tragedy warns against hubris. Comedy reminds us of the funny creatures we actually are, as distinct from the grandiose images we emulate at our peril. As a whole, I believe that the arts have a tendency to make us somewhat better, or if not better at least to avoid the worse within ourselves. There are exceptions and I have dwelt on the most glaring one. Wagner was not a warning against hubris but a product of the greatest wave of hubris that has swept a culture in modern times. He was also the chief inspiration of the most horrendous case of hubris to erupt in modern history. But it is reasonable to hope that the Wagner-Hitler relation will remain forever exceptional: not necessarily aberrant, just exceptional. Let it serve as a salutary reminder of the dire possibilities that can lurk within even the performing arts, both in the wider and in the narrower sense.

Let me close on the theme of the containment, rather than elimination, of destructive forces. The great exemplification of this, in dramatic art, is of course the *Oresteia* of Aeschylus. The goddess Athena sets out to break the cycle of blood feud, by containing the Furies. She does not rebuke them but treats them with respect, even with a degree of deference. They are not to have Orestes, who is their chosen prey and, as they believe, their destined due. Orestes must be spared: on that, the goddess demands obedience. The Furies are thereby reminded of a higher power than theirs. But their nature is not changed, nor are they stripped of all jurisdiction. They are to have an honoured place, a temple within the city. The destructive forces are not eliminated; they are contained.

The clear-eyed goddess does not contemplate any Utopia, for we are not fit for such, but she does show how, with calm and prudent management, the better can sometimes get the better of the worse. In the austerity of its limitation, this is one of the greatest moments in the history of art and of civilization.

I would like to think that the spirit of the *Oresteia* will dominate the coming century and extend to permeate the third millennium. Unfortunately, there are a number of signs to the contrary.*

---

* This chapter is partly based on my keynote address "A World Falling Apart" to the 1994 annual convention of the International Society of Performing Arts Administrators in Sydney Opera House.

IV
THE
MILLENNIUM
COMMISSION

OUR PRESENT PERIOD — nearing the halfway mark of the final decade of the twentieth century — might be described as the dawn of the eve of the millennium. Few people seem, as yet, to be preoccupied with the impending epochal date. Australia is an exception, but that is because the Olympic Games are scheduled for Sydney in the year 2000.

Still, in some quarters there is already an urge to do something about the coming event, in a more general sort of way. The British government, in February 1994, set up a ten-member body with the portentous title "The Millennium Commission." The terms of reference of this body seem to be remarkably vague. All I know about it — and I should imagine about all that most people in Britain know about it — is contained in an article by Marianne Macdonald which appeared in the London *Independent on Sunday* on 18 September 1994. According to Ms. Macdonald, Peter Brooke, the secretary of state for national heritage, who set up the commission, said that the commission is looking for "exceptionally distinctive proposals that are 'of the millennium.'"

"Of the millennium" has a fine ring to it. But what does it mean? What Brooke, personally, may have meant by it might possibly have become clear in practice, for when he coined the phrase, he expected to be presiding over the Millennium Commission in his governmental capacity. However, he personally ceased to be "of the millennium" as a result of being fired by John Major in a cabinet reshuffle shortly after he set up the commission. Brooke's successor, Stephen Dorrell, also succeeded him as chairman of the commission. If the present chairman of the commission knows what is meant by "of the millennium," he is not telling us. Marianne Macdonald writes:

> The commission has been told to approve projects which are "of the millennium," but members admitted last week to being unable to define the phrase; and on Friday, the Secretary of State for National Heritage, Stephen Dorrell, who chairs the commission, said he had no plans to clarify it.

One wonders what the chairman of the commission *has* plans for, then.

Ms. Macdonald went on to question three other members of the commission — Simon Jenkins, Michael Montague, and Heather Couper — about "of the millennium." Their combined answers add nothing to the blank registered by their chairman. As Ms. Macdonald reports:

> Simon Jenkins, former editor of the *Times*, said last

week: "You've put your finger on the problem, which is, what is 'of the millennium'?"

Michael Montague, former chairman of the English Tourist Board, called it "intangible," while the astronomer Professor Heather Couper, on being told that people were confused, said: "So are we."

Quite so. As none of the interviewed members of the British Millennium Commission is prepared even to attempt an answer to the question, let me offer my own definition. *Of the millennium*: A term without any specific cognitive or conceptual connotation; employed, like terms in advertising, to evoke favourable associations with regard to a particular project or product; the particular favourable associations which this particular term is designed to evoke are those which used to be evoked by such terms as the American "with it" or the French "*à la page*" or "*dans le mouvement*"; *functionally*, the term is designed as a certificate of high fashion to be awarded to approved British projects and products in the closing years of the twentieth century and the opening years of the twenty-first; the certificate will accompany and appear to validate the allocation of large sums of money, out of lottery funds.

My definition would be perfectly intelligible at any convention of the advertising profession. But it would not sound well on the lips of a member of a body with such a solemn-sounding and apparently inspirational title as the Millennium Commission. Hence I believe the obvious embarrassment and confusion of members of the commission, when asked what "of the millennium" meant. What it means is so frivolous and so vapid that to acknowledge it explicitly would demolish the reputations for seriousness which earned the members their seats. That might be a very good thing, but the members of the commission may be forgiven for failing to view the matter in that light.

There are other curious things about the commission, and I suspect that all these may be connected with a wider malaise in Western culture near the close of the second millennium. I shall be coming back later to that larger theme. For the moment, I shall be taking a last look at the commission with regard to its relation to the spiritual and intellectual spheres.

In her article, Macdonald says of the commission: "Their problem will be deciding just what is suitable to mark the beginning of the third millennium after Christ." Yet none of the commission members whom that reporter interviewed is recorded as having made the slightest reference to the existence of such a problem. None of them alludes to Christ, Christianity, Christians, or the Christian Era. Nor do they even show any sign of interest in the idea of the millennium, either as a spiritual or an historical phenomenon. All they are interested in seems to be the end of this century and the beginning of the next. "Millennium" seems to be for them no more than a fancy designation, with significant promotional possibilities, which happens to attach to the end of our present century.

It seems strange that there should apparently be no Christian dimension to the contemplation by the British Millennium Commission of an event whose primary significance is the closing of one division of the Christian Era and the opening of a third. It seems especially strange that this should be so in Britain which — unlike the United States — is technically a Christian country. Unlike the U.S., Britain has an established church, or rather two established churches, the Church of England and the Church of Scotland, of both of which the British monarch is head. The bishops of the Church of England sit, *ex officio*, in the Parliament of the United Kingdom, which set up the commission.

So, for the Millennium Commission to be apparently oblivious of the Christian import of what is for Christians primarily a Christian event, is a phenomenon which seems to require some accounting for.

It is true that the ostensible and ostentatious Christianity of the British Constitution involves large amounts of hypocrisy. True also that *all* forms of social organization involve sizeable amounts of hypocrisy. Hypocrisy indeed is inseparable from all forms of social life. No one can live with a really determined and consistent enemy of all hypocrisy. Molière made that point in *Le Misanthrope*, and Ibsen in *The Wild Duck*. In the twentieth century Simone Weil rejected the teachings of Molière and Ibsen as corrupting. She insisted on nothing but the truth, in her writings and in her personal life. Her most famous statement was a declaration of total disseverance, a rejection of all bonding. Said Weil: "Any sentence that begins with the word 'We' is a lie." It was a lie that she refused to tell.

Nobody can live like that, and Weil willed her own

death. She was tubercular while serving with the Free French forces in Britain during the Second World War, and she killed herself by refusing the special rations to which she was entitled as a tubercular person. Her action was posthumously seen as one of solidarity with the people of occupied France, then undergoing a more severe regime of rationing. But solidarity is hardly her thing. I see her action as essentially a rejection of the people among whom she had chosen to live, and among whom she could not bear to live. Rejection, because of the hypocrisy of those people, their compromises, their childish and bonding nationalisms, their constant use of sentences beginning with "we," and their general human mediocrity and awfulness.

We cannot, then, live without at least a modicum of hypocrisy. There are times, however, when the hypocrisy of a given society reaches such a level that it brims over, arousing general disgust, followed by the collapse or mutation of the society in question. That happened in pre-Reformation Europe. It happened again in the France of the *ancien régime* in the decades before the French Revolution. And it happened in our own time, in the former Soviet Union, on the eve of the collapse of Communism. And something like that may now be happening in contemporary Britain as well as in other parts of the West.

I know it is likely to sound extravagant to suggest that change of such a cosmic kind may be about to happen in the humdrum conditions of the Britain of Queen Elizabeth II, John Major, and the Millennium Commission. It is human to be reassured by the humdrum. The early stages of what we can see in retrospect as preludes of revolutionary change *are* humdrum. Life in Paris was pretty humdrum, politically speaking, around 1755. By 1765 it was no longer so, but already seething with discontent. And that was a generation before the actual Revolution.

Stendhal has written of what he calls the *crystallization* of a loving relationship. André Gide, commenting on Stendhal, concentrates on the *decrystallization* of love. Something analogous happens within societies and states when they begin to fall out of love with themselves. When decrystallization, or disenchantment, sets in, it is the prelude — quite often a prolonged one — to revolution. Conventions and practices which had once been contemplated with pride and affection, and were a source of collective reassurance, gradually begin to look tawdry, obsolete, a source of collective embarrassment. That happened to the relationship between the French people, on the one hand, and the monarchy and the Catholic Church, on the other, in the late eighteenth century. I suspect that something similar may be happening to the relation between the British people, on the one hand, and the British monarchy and the established churches, on the other, as we near the end of the twentieth century and of the second millennium of the Christian Era.

It is in that context that this curious institution, the British Millennium Commission, takes on some symptomatic epochal significance. Symptomatic because of the apparent deficiency in its membership of a sense of history and a capacity for awe. Now, unless contemplated with such a sense and such a capacity, the constitutional Christian monarchy and the established churches are merely vestigial phenomena to be tidied away as soon as possible. Since a capacity for awe and a sense of history are important to the preservation of the British Constitution — as is clearly the case — one would think that the celebration of the closing of the second millennium of the Christian Era, and the opening of the third, would have been seen in Britain as an occasion preeminently requiring the exercise of that capacity and that sense. After all, both the history and the future of the monarchy and the churches and of much else are deeply involved.

Against that background, one might expect the commission to include poets and other artists; philosophers, both of religious and secular tendencies; and historians, both of religion and of society in general. Not at all. No persons belonging to any of these categories has a seat. The commission is made up of businessmen, politicians, and charity organizers, plus one journalist, one astronomer, one lawyer (a black woman and therefore a mandatory twofer), and one veteran of assorted quangos. That last member is nominated by the opposition; the others are all the choices of Her Majesty's government.

The reported utterances of the members of the commission are resolutely trendy and guaranteed free from awe and sense of history: at least history on the scale of the millennium. The most articulate member is, as might be expected, the journalist. Simon Jenkins, the former editor of *The Times*, is said to hope for some project that "in some way marks the passage of the century either monumentally or conceptually." This seems a remarkably limited objective, temporally speaking, for a member of something called the Millennium Commission. But then the idea of a millennium is something awkward to handle, for the trendily disposed. Easier to think about what may look fashionable in six years' time. Sorry, not just fashionable: "of the millennium."

"We don't want old projects," said Simon Jenkins, speaking for the members of the Millennium Commission. "We want fizz, excitement, panache."

Macdonald says that "one of the best proposals floated so far must be the architect David Marks's idea for a Ferris wheel on the site of the Jubilee Gardens standing 200ft above Big Ben."

The style of the reported utterances of the commission members puts me in mind of the recorded utterances of *habitués* of the Paris salons circa 1765. Those smart people too were obsessed with being *à la mode*, agog for gimmickry, contemptuous of the past and unaware of its weight over the future, altogether free from awe and effortlessly contemptuous of all persons in any way disposed to barbarous emotions of that kind. The sophisticated *abbés* who flitted from salon to salon during that confident and ominous period were not hypocrites, though they belonged to a church establishment which was, as they assured their friends, a monument of total hypocrisy. But these *abbés* were something much more dangerous. They were people who had lost sight of the social importance of the institution they were supposed to be hypocritical about.

Years later, after the great revolution of whose coming these sophisticated intellectuals had not the slightest inkling, the poet Alfred de Musset apostrophized the great mentor and exemplar of all these people, in the following words:

Ris-donc Voltaire! Ris-donc, que ton hideux sourire
Voltige encore sur tes os décharnés!
Il est tombé sur nous, cet édifice immense
Que de tes larges mains tu sapais nuit et jour.

It doesn't go very well into English, but let me offer a literal translation:

Laugh on, Voltaire, laugh on!
Let your hideous smile flit yet once more over your
    fleshless bones!
It has fallen on us, that immense edifice
Which you undermined with your large hands, by day
    and by night.

Neither Voltaire nor his imitators had any intention of undermining the whole *ancien régime* (whatever their intentions for the Church). The type of British establishment figure I have been talking about has no intention of undermining the British constitutional monarchy. Yet the undermining is going on and these people are contributing to it — by assigning low value to the ideas and emotions which have sustained the monarchy. The low value which they assign to these things would normally be inconspicuous. As it happens, it is the coming of the millennium, and the emergence of that egregious Millennium Commission, which have caused this anomaly within the contemporary British value system to stand out, at least to my eye.

"We don't want old projects," said one member of the commission. Well, the British monarchy, whatever else it may be, is certainly an old project. So it has been served notice that it is decidedly not "of the millennium." A crushing verdict, it would appear, even if no one on the commission seems to know what it means.

Perhaps some of those with authority in Britain will give some rather more profound attention to these matters in the years between now and the year 2000 itself?

In the next part of my remarks, I want to devote some thought to the future of the British monarchy in the opening period of the third millennium of the Christian Era. But before that, I need to refer to a general point which may be puzzling a class of people to whom I owe special consideration. I mean those who have been following attentively to this point. Some, probably most, will be concerned about what may well appear to be a major inconsistency within the series. Earlier — especially in relation to America — I wrote of the Enlightenment tradition with great respect. Yet just now I wrote slightingly of the *habitués* of the Paris salons of the late eighteenth century. But were not those same *habitués* the most energetic propagators of Enlightenment values in their own day? They were indeed, but they were the propagators of *a particular version* of Enlightenment values. The Enlightenment they represented was radically innovative, contemptuous of tradition, bitterly and contemptuously hostile of Christianity, and having as its hallmark an overbearing and universally meddlesome frivolity.

The earlier Enlightenment — the Enlightenment of Locke and Montesquieu — was not like that. The mainstream Enlightenment tradition, in England and Scotland and North America, has never been like that. The Enlightenment tradition of the English-speaking world is one which has coexisted, amicably but never uncritically, with religion. Edmund Burke, who belonged in that tradition, watched the progress of the French Enlightenment in the second half of the eighteenth century with deep foreboding. As early as 1756, Burke warned, in a tract called *A Vindication of Natural Society*, that the attempt to uproot religion would result also in political and social revolution. The warning was ignored. Burke's prediction came true in 1789, thirty-three years after it was made.

If Burke were alive today and learned of the spirit in which the close of the second millennium of the Christian Era is about to be celebrated by members of the British Millennium Commission, he would be entertaining forebodings about the future of Britain similar to the ones he entertained about the future of France more than a generation before the French Revolution. Paradoxically, the commission's ardent and frivolous pursuit of novelty for its own sake is carrying it back more than two hundred years, to the *Siècle de Lumière*. The style of Louis XV is "of the millennium."

So, then, how long may the British monarchy be expected to last into the third millennium of the Christian Era?

Before attempting to answer that one, it is well to reflect a little on an even more venerable institution, the papacy. Throughout the second half of the second millennium of the Christian Era, there have been people, in every generation, who confidently expected the papacy's imminent demise. The confidence came in waves. The early Protestants were perhaps the most confident of all, and certainly the most fervent in their confidence. Their hopes declined amidst the grisly stalemate of the religious wars, and the project of the abolition of the papacy was indefinitely postponed by the Peace of Westphalia in 1648.

Yet the expectation of the papacy's demise, unlike the Protestant project for its forcible abolition, stayed around; in this, indeed, resembling the papacy itself. Most of the thinkers of the eighteenth-century Enlightenment — especially in its late French phase — expected that the Enlightenment itself, the progress of *les Lumières*, would simply cause the papacy to fade away, like all the dark unhappy past. Voltaire's approach was more activist — *écrasez l'infâme*: squash the infamous thing! The French Revolution, elevating Voltaire to the Pantheon, inherited that project but failed to carry it through.

The Emperor Napoleon, most pragmatic of the children of the Enlightenment, decided that a deal with the papacy would on the whole be good, rather than bad, for the morale of his troops, so he cut the deal. He

thought of himself as having the pope in his pocket —
and so he had, for the duration.

That is, *his* duration. But the papacy, as an institution,
outlived the emperor, his pocket, and his empire. The
papacy became a pillar of the Holy Alliance, the new
European order which arose on the ruins of the French
Revolution and the Napoleonic Empire. And then the
papacy outlived the Holy Alliance, and after that the
European revolutions of 1848. The papacy's greatest
trauma was the unification of Italy against the will of
the papacy and at the expense of its temporal power,
in 1870. But if we look at the state of Italy, on the eve
of the third millennium, we have to see that the papacy
looks like lasting longer into that millennium than
does a unified Italy.

In the twentieth century, the papacy has survived
both the Russian Empire and the Soviet Union. In
surviving the latter it also survived the Marxist system
which had predicted, with an air of scientific infallibil-
ity, the inevitable disappearance of such religious ves-
tiges. It has survived the Hohenzollern and the
Hapsburg empires. It has survived Hitler's Thousand
Year Reich. And it has survived the British and French
empires.

To contemplate the papacy of our own day, standing
as it does amidst the detritus of five centuries of failed
predictions about its demise, must inhibit even the bold-
est against predicting the demise of any ancient institution. Before I proceed, nonetheless, to discuss the future
of the British monarchy, into the next millennium, I need
to say something about the nature of prediction.

The nature of my present undertaking — considering matters arising on the eve of the millennium — does not indeed require of me absolutely that I should predict, or purport to predict. But it does require of me that I should try to look forward through the swirling mists that must surround even the opening years of the next millennium, as well as backward into the historical record of the millennium that is now about to expire.

Even looking backward requires a lot of guesswork. There is more guesswork in historiography than the more confidently document-reliant schools of historians can readily admit. Billions and billions of transactions must have occurred in the course of what we, rather presumptuously, call "recorded history." But of all those billions of transactions, only a tiny proportion has left any record. And even what does survive is as likely to be intended to deceive as to illuminate.

Pretty well everything that has been preserved "for the record," with the instruction of posterity consciously in mind, is riddled with *suppressio veri* and *suggestio falsi*, tending to the glorification of the interests which caused the document to be prepared, and to the vilification of their enemies.

Historians, in examining such documents, look for the bits that are *not* intended for posterity, but which are there because they were generally known to, and taken for granted by, contemporaries. And the documents which historians most prize are those written down with no thought of posterity in mind but solely for an immediate mundane and practical purpose. And such documents have been preserved only spottily and by chance, for the earlier part of the millennium now expiring. For the later part, especially for the last hundred and fifty years, the problem is the sheer abundance of the documents.

So even the historian must do a lot of guessing. Or if you prefer more scientific-sounding language, the historian must often elaborate hypotheses which are not fully capable of empirical verification.

So much for the past. When we are attempting to look at the future of human societies — in, for example, the opening years of the next millennium — it is almost entirely a matter of guesswork. I am not even sure about the "almost," but let me hazard that qualifier.

In the natural sciences, of course, precise prediction is often possible. Thus there is only one member of that Millennium Commission who will be able to inform her colleagues with something resembling certainty of a number of events which will take place in the course of the third millennium. I refer of course to the astronomer member, Professor Heather Couper, who is described as co-author of *The Halley's Comet Pop-Up Book*. But the recently observed behaviour of certain comets reminds us that even astronomers do not know for sure whether the planet we now inhabit will still be there by the end of the third millennium. At some point during that thousand-year span, the papacy may have to find out whether it can survive without a planet.

As regards the future of human societies, with such an enormous number of complex variables, we are reduced almost entirely to guessing. Still, there have been some few who have understood the nature of their own times so well that they have been able to draw inferences from their knowledge which had a predictive character, above and beyond mere guesswork.

Paradoxically, three of the most successful seers in that line (though still only partially successful) in the first half of the twentieth century were followers of Karl Marx: that is to say, persons burdened with the most absurdly flawed collection of predictions that has been vouchsafed to any thinker since Nostradamus. But Lenin, Trotsky, and Stalin used their knowledge of Marxist theory and Marxist dialectics more to dazzle their followers, and confound their opponents, within the revolutionary movement, than to determine their own choices, in any practical conjuncture of importance. Their *Das Kapital* was like Oliver Cromwell's Bible: it meant what they decided it should mean, when the chips were down.

Lenin's great predictive intuition, in the circumstances of late 1917, was that the party which would opt unhesitatingly for peace at any price, with the Central Powers, could win and hold power over Russia with the help of the most active elements in the mutinous soldiery. Trotsky got that one wrong — with his theory of "neither war nor peace" — and Lenin overruled him.

Stalin's speciality, as regards capacity for prediction by inference, lay in his understanding of national and ethnic rivalries, and of dynastic and class aspects of these rivalries. Out of these, he evolved a theory of nationalities, supposedly based on the writings of Marx, who in reality made even less sense on the subject of nationalities than on other subjects. But Stalin's theory was only protective adaptation to a dominant jargon. His genius lay in the practice whereby, through a ruthless and at the same time subtle application of his knowledge and intuition in the field of nationalities, he recuperated for the Bolsheviks — and later for himself personally — almost all of the former Empire of the Tsars of All the Russias.

Trotsky, who took Marx and Engels more seriously than either Lenin or Stalin did, got his practical inferences proportionately more wrong than they did and, unlike them, was driven from power and into exile. But in exile he did get one big thing right that Stalin got wrong. In the late 1920s and early 1930s, Stalin ordered the German Communists to fight the Social Democrats and ignore the National Socialists, who, being mere reactionaries, would fade away by the laws of history. Trotsky, on the other hand, understood the furious dynamism of Hitler's movement, well before it came to power in Germany, and inferred the future out of that understanding. "If Fascism comes to power in Germany," he warned the working class, "it will jolt over your skulls and spines like a tremendous tank."

Each of those three got one big predictive inference right, but each also got others wrong. Other major figures of the twentieth century — including Hitler and Churchill — have a rather similar predictive track record.

I know of only one instance in history where a statesman and political thinker had such an insight into the greatest political phenomenon of his time as to enable him to predict its major events with consistent accuracy. I refer to Edmund Burke and the French Revolution.

As we saw, Burke had foreseen, more than thirty years ahead of the event, that the undermining of religion must result in political and social revolution. When the event arrived in July 1789, Burke predicted its course, with the same accuracy. By the late summer of 1789, the conventional wisdom, both in France and in Britain, was that the revolution was, to all intents and purposes, over. Burke's friend, William Windham — who had been in Paris in late August and early September 1789 — reported to Burke on September 15 in an optimistic strain: "My prediction was (and accounts which I heard since my being there have contributed to confirm it) that they would very soon become perfectly orderly."

In his reply, dated September 27, Burke makes short work of poor Windham's prediction. Of the French revolutionary leadership of this period — the generation of Lafayette — Burke wrote:

> I very much question, whether they are in a condition
> to exercise any function of decided authority — or
> even whether they are possessed of any real
> deliberative capacity, or the exercise of free Judgement
> in any point whatsoever; as there is a Mob of their
> constituents ready to Hang them if They should
> deviate into moderation, or in the least depart from the
> Spirit of those they represent.

All Burke's contemporaries and friends would have regarded that as a very crude interpretation of some highly complex matters. But events of just ten days later demonstrated that Windham had got it wrong and Burke had got it right. In the revolutionary *Journées* of 5-6 October, a crowd of 30,000 Parisians, men and women, marched from Paris to Versailles and abducted the royal family, bringing them back with them to Paris. Lafayette and friends followed what Burke had called "the Mob of their constituents" out to Versailles, where Lafayette advised the king to do what the mob wanted, and then accompanied them back to Paris.

The year 1790, in which Burke wrote *Reflections on the Revolution in France*, was the quietest full year in the whole history of the French Revolution. Again virtually everybody, except Burke, believed, as Windham had in 1789, before the October days, that the revolution, as a violent set of upheavals, was over. Burke knew it was not and said so in *Reflections*. I once taught that book to an undergraduate class at New York University. Undergraduates are often vague about dates and I found that my class, while reading *Reflections*, assumed that when that book was written the bloodiest events of the revolution — the September Massacres, the executions of the king and queen, the Terror — had already happened. In reality all those events lay in the future when Burke was writing *Reflections*. Burke sensed them as latent in the general conditions which he had described to Windham in September 1789: which conditions continued to prevail in Paris beneath the tranquil surface which was all that other people saw, in 1790-91.

The period 1790-91 was one of constitution-making in Paris. The new constitution — which in theory reinforced a constitutional monarchy — was greatly admired by fashionable and liberal people of the time. Charles James Fox, in a House of Commons debate on 15 April 1791, declared that he admired "the new constitution of France, taken together, as the most stupendous and glorious edifice of liberty, which had been erected on the foundation of human integrity in any time or country." Fox was at this time the leader of the Whig Party in the Commons, and Burke was the most prominent member of that party, next to Fox. Burke now broke with Fox and the Whigs, over the French Revolution in general, but specifically over what he regarded as Fox's preposterous tribute to the French constitution.

Burke saw the French constitutional monarchy as a total fraud, since the supposed constitutional monarch was actually a prisoner of the legislative branch, with at their backs "a Mob of their constituents ready to Hang them if they should deviate into moderation. . . ."

The Whigs, that April, contemptuously denied that Louis XVI was a prisoner. But two months later Louis himself proved the Whigs wrong, and Burke right, by attempting to escape from his captivity, getting as far as Varennes and being forcibly brought back by those who had held him and his family captive since October. Even after the return from Varennes, the farce of the constitutional monarchy was kept up. But not for long.

In September, the captive king formally swore allegiance to the constitution devised by his captors. From afar, the English Whigs duly applauded this edifying scene. Less than a year later, on 10 August 1792, the Paris mob, summoned by Danton and the Commune, purged the National Assembly, deposed the king, and tore up the Constitution of 1791. "The most stupendous edifice of liberty" etc. was no more, after less than a year of formal existence.

Burke had foreseen the transit of power within the revolution that occurred in August 1792. In *Letter to a Member of the National Assembly*, written in January 1791 — well before even the king's flight to Varennes — he contrasted the types of revolutionary then nominally in charge with the types which would succeed them. Of the first he wrote:

> They are men who would usurp the government of their country with decency and moderation. In fact, they are nothing more or better than men engaged in desperate designs with feeble minds. They are not honest; they are only ineffectual and unsystematic in their iniquity. They are persons who want not the dispositions, but the energy and vigor that is necessary for great evil machinations.

Burke goes on:

> But these men naturally are despised by those who have heads to know, and hearts that are able to go through the necessary demands of bold, wicked enterprises. They

are naturally classed below the latter description, and will only be used by them as inferior instruments. They will be only the Fairfaxes of your Cromwells.

In this same *Letter*, Burke specifically predicts the execution of the king — "assassination," as he calls it, consistently with his view of the transaction in question. Burke wrote:

> Nothing that I can say, or that you can say, will hasten them [the Revolutionaries], by a single hour, in the execution of a design which they have long since entertained. In spite of their solemn declarations, their soothing addresses, and the multiplied oaths which they have taken and forced others to take, they will assassinate the king when his name will no longer be necessary to their designs; but not a moment sooner.

That was written in January 1791, when Louis XVI was still girt with all the trappings of a constitutional monarch, and when no one but Burke saw him as in any danger. The king was executed two years later. Burke also predicted the assassination of the queen. She was executed in October 1793.

The most remarkable of all Burke's accurate predictions was the passage in *Reflections on the Revolution in France* in which he described how the French Revolution would eventually be brought to an end:

> It is known that armies have hitherto yielded a very precarious and uncertain obedience to any senate or

popular authority; and they will least of all yield it to
an Assembly which is to have only a continuance of
two years. The officers must totally lose the
characteristic disposition of military men, if they see
with perfect submission and due admiration the
dominion of pleaders; especially when they find that
they have a new court to pay to an endless succession
of those pleaders, whose military policy, and the
genius of whose command, (if they should have any),
must be as uncertain as their duration is transient. In
the weakness of one kind of authority, and in the
fluctuation of all, the officers of an army will remain
for some time mutinous and full of faction, until some
popular general, who understands the art of
conciliating the soldiery, and who possesses the true
spirit of command, shall draw the eyes of all men upon
himself. Armies will obey him on his personal account.
There is no other way of securing military obedience in
this state of things. But the moment in which that event
shall happen, the person who really commands the
army is your master; the master (that is little) of your
king, the master of your Assembly, the master of your
whole republic.

The seizure of power by Napoleon Bonaparte — the
great event inferred by Burke out of his unrivalled
understanding of the French Revolution — occurred
on 18 Brumaire (9 November) 1799, nine years after the
publication of *Reflections*, and more than two years
after the death of its author.

Burke's astonishing capacity to see into the ways in

which events were moving derived not from any mystical intuition but from penetrating powers of observation, judicious inference from what was observed, and thorough analysis of what was discerned by observation and inference.

It is your misfortune, and mine also, that Burke is not available to deliver these Massey Lectures around the theme "On the Eve of the Millennium." What a *régale* that would have been! What you have to make do with instead are the reflections of a student and devotee of Burke, attempting to grapple with the theme of the millennium in a Burkean spirit, which is definitely not "of the millennium" in the contemporary London sense.

I am well aware that any personal predictive capacities I may have are far from being in the Burkean league, and I shall therefore be fairly tentative in seeking to infer from present conditions what the transition from millennium to millennium may hold for us. All the same, I should like to hazard some thoughts within that general framework, about a particular subject which we have been skirting from time to time since the beginning of this lecture: the future of the British monarchy.

I doubt whether the monarchy can survive until the end of the next century. And I fear that its disappearance may wrench the fabric of British society in such a way as to endanger British democracy and even — in conjunction with other forces — endanger democracy in the West in general.

As we have seen, the survival of the papacy, against

all apparent odds, should put us on our guard against predicting the demise of ancient institutions. Yet the two cases are not closely comparable. The papacy has always been *primarily* a spiritual institution, the British monarchy *primarily* a political one. The British monarchy is primarily a national institution; its Imperial, and later its Commonwealth role, being secondary. The papacy antedates the creation of nation-states, and since such states came into being, the papacy has been primarily an international spiritual institution and sometimes a supranational one.

A spiritual and international institution has certain advantages, in point of durability, over a political and national one, however venerable. A spiritual institution offers rewards, and threatens punishments; both sets to be awarded or inflicted in the hereafter. So those who yearn for the rewards and dread the punishments have no means of verifying, here below, whether the threats and the promises have any basis in reality. This gives the spiritual institution a very high degree of immunity from blame, a condition highly conducive to survival.

A political institution, on the other hand, must show positive, tangible results, right here below, or be blamed for failure. A constitutional monarchy, it is true, does not have to take the blame for the failure of any particular government. But if, under a number of successive governments, but under the same monarchy, there is a succession of setbacks, the monarchy cannot ultimately escape some share of the blame.

Similarly, an established international institution

has major terrestrial advantages over every national one. Specifically, the papacy, after it had been relieved of the burden of its temporal power in 1870, was able to enjoy the huge advantage of neutrality in both world wars, since its spiritual subjects were among the nationals of all belligerents. The British monarchy, being a national institution, was a belligerent from beginning to end of both wars. Those wars brought glory and victory to Britain and enhanced the monarchy in the hour of victory. But their cost was extremely heavy both in lives and resources, resulting in a slow but serious decline in Britain's international standing.

Inevitably, that decline has been accompanied by a decline in the prestige of the monarchy. The depth of that decline can be registered by comparing the status of the throne today with its status exactly one hundred years ago, six years after Queen Victoria's Golden Jubilee and three years before her Diamond Jubilee. The monarchy of the late twentieth century is, and can only be, a shadow of what it was in the late nineteenth century.

Nor is it just a question of a decline in prestige, serious though that is for any monarchy. Among the resources squandered in the two world wars were some intangible resources needful to the lives of monarchies. I have made allusion to some of these earlier. They include awe, a sense of national history, and of pride in national history; also the general assumption of deference to one's social superiors: an assumption common among all classes a hundred years ago and tending to sustain the monarch at the apex of the social pyramid.

All these attitudes and assumptions were grievously impaired by the horrendous impact of the First World War. Some of them seemed to be significantly rehabilitated by the Second World War, and the general admiration and affection for the essentially Victorian figure of Winston Churchill. But the discarding of Churchill by the electorate immediately after the war demonstrated that the attitudes and assumptions impaired by the first war had never really recovered. That could be seen as ominous, in a general way, for the future of the monarchy. Yet, though shorn of some of its beams, the monarchy still seemed secure enough, from the happy coronation of Queen Elizabeth II to the penultimate decade of the twentieth century.

It is in our own time, the last two decades of the twentieth century, that the corrosive effects of the changes in the value system began to eat into the royal family itself, causing serious questions about its future to be asked and pondered more seriously than ever before.

The long-term decline in deference which had set in within the culture in the second decade of the twentieth century began to accelerate in the last decades of our century, the eve of the millennium.

In large part, this was a result of what has been called the communications revolution, and in particular the intense competition between mass-circulation newspapers specializing in the emotional stimulation of the barely literate. It was discovered that the private lives, and especially the sex lives, of easily recognizable members of the royal family were a major marketable resource. This resource was therefore exploited with words and pictures — especially pictures — through various combinations of prurience, envy, and resentment, and in other forms of gloating at the shameful details of lives of the high and mighty, the privileged and the attractive.

I need not dwell on the general character of these recent developments. They are only too well known to all of us. I should just like to take up two points, with regard to them, which have a significant specific bearing on the future of the monarchy.

The first is, that this line of development is almost certainly irreversible. Members of the royal family who are in any way vulnerable will continue to be wounded by the tabloids throughout what is left of the present century and millennium and well into the next. Early in the present decade, indeed, resentment among the middle and upper classes at the hounding of royals by the tabloids induced John Major's government to consider legislation which would drastically penalize intrusions into privacy. When a member of Mr. Major's government made an announcement to that effect, and issued a public warning to the tabloids — "Last Chance Saloon" — disaster struck immediately. The minister concerned was forced to resign as a result of highly embarrassing revelations, courtesy of the tabloids, about his personal sex life. Other politicians, in all parties, trembled as skeletons rattled throughout the cupboards of Westminster.

Nothing more was ever heard about the drastic legislation which was to curb the power of the tabloids. That incident has chilling implications, not only for the future of the British monarchy, but for the future of democracy itself, and not only in Britain.

The second feature which has a bearing on the future of the monarchy concerns the person of the monarch. Queen Elizabeth II is universally respected, altogether untouched by scandal, endowed with an aura of invulnerability, as she nears the end of her long reign. Her successors are unlikely to inherit that enviable armour. At some point in the next century, the ravenous and now irrepressible scandalmongering of the mass-circulation press is bound to fasten on the monarch in person. Fasten, and not let go. And the appetite of the scandalmongers will not be sated by the fall of just *one* monarch.

For these reasons, I think it unlikely that the British monarchy can survive to the end of the next century. Its fall will have very serious implications, not only for Britain, but also for the whole of the West.

In Britain, the crisis over the monarchy, which is bound to be a prolonged one, must pose a threat to the survival of the whole political system based, as it has been for more than three hundred years, on the principle of constitutional monarchy. Bear in mind that the allegiance of the armed forces is to the hereditary crown, not to any Parliament-without-the-crown, still less to the House of Commons alone, and least of all to some general ideas about democracy. Burke's warning about the instability of "a dominion of pleaders" is

relevant here. As regards the specifically British consequences of all this, I must stop there. One must not
pile prediction upon prediction.

As regards the wider implications for the West, that
is a very large subject which I must reserve, with other
related matter, for my final chapter, which will consider the general prospects for Western values into the
third millennium.

Let me close with a brief note on the impact of
pornography on politics, a theme suggested by the
treatment of the British royals at the hands of the
tabloids.

Pornography has the power to delegitimize, by
stripping the high ones of respect and exposing them
to contempt. Pornography, customarily regarded as
apolitical, has therefore an enormous revolutionary
potential.

This was demonstrated more than two hundred
years ago in the sources of the archetypical revolution
of modern times. Much ink has been spilt on the intellectual origins of the French Revolution. Much less has
been heard about that revolution's *pornographic* origins. The intellectual origins were, it is true, extremely
important in the long run, as Burke had seen. But on
the eve of the revolution itself, in the 1780s, the business end of the pre-revolutionary process was in the
hands of the pornographers. The favourite reading of
Parisians in those years consisted of *les libelles*. These
were pornographic pamphlets, clandestinely published or illegally imported, but widely available and
exclusively directed at the supposed sex-life of the

French royal family, and of Marie Antoinette in particular. These fascinatingly smutty little booklets — which could be read aloud to the illiterate — did much to shape the attitudes of the Paris mob towards the royal family: a major factor at various stages of the revolution.

Nor did the revolutionary leaders scorn the revolutionary potential of the pornographic *libelles*. From these was drawn the last but not the least deadly in the Articles of Charge against Marie Antoinette which led to her execution in October 1793. "Oh God!" wrote Edmund Burke, "the Charge! and the last article particularly!" This stated that Marie Antoinette "had committed indecencies with her son, too shocking to mention."

One of the things that can safely be predicted about the opening decades of the third millennium is that pornography — through video and otherwise — will greatly increase in availability, audacity, and influence. That it will rise in public esteem seems probable. In its more novel forms it is trendy. It certainly has "excitement, fizz"; perhaps it is even achieving "panache" by now. In terms of the values cherished by the British Millennium Commission, pornography is most definitely "of the millennium."

V
THE
GUARDED PALACE

EVEN BEFORE THE OPENING of the last quarter of the twentieth century, my imagination was at grips with the idea of what the world would be like at the end of the century. Specifically, I was concerned with the moral and ethical consequences, for the advanced world, of what its relations would then be with the poor world. In an essay on Friedrich Nietzsche entitled "The Gentle Nietzscheans," published in *The New York Review of Books* in November 1970, I referred to what I called "historical reasons why a Nietzschean ethic may come to recommend itself." I went on:

> The world by the turn of the century is likely to present some terrible aspects. The comfortable countries, if they can keep their hands off one another's throats, will be more comfortable, or at least more affluent than ever. But the poor world is likely to be drowning in the excess of its own population, a human swirl of self-destructive currents, of which the Nigeria-Biafra war may have been a type and forerunner.

Let me interrupt that quotation there to refer to a whole

chain of later similar events, most recently in Somalia,
Rwanda, and Haiti. In that 1970 essay, I continued:

> The advanced world may well be like, and feel like, a
> closed and guarded palace, in a city gripped by the
> plague. There is another metaphor, developed by
> André Gide, one of the many powerful minds
> powerfully influenced by Nietzsche: This is the
> metaphor of the lifeboat, in a sea full of the survivors
> of a shipwreck. The hands of survivors cling to the
> sides of the boat. But the boat has already as many
> passengers as it can carry. No more survivors can be
> accommodated, and if they gather and cling on, the
> boat will sink and all be drowned. The captain orders
> out the hatchets. The hands of the survivors are
> severed. The lifeboat and its passengers are saved.
>
> Something like this is the logic we apply, when we
> tighten our immigration laws, and in the general
> pattern of our relations with the so-called
> under-developed countries. . . . As this situation
> becomes more obvious it is likely to generate its own
> psychological and moral pressures. The traditional
> ethic will require larger and larger doses of its
> traditional built-in antidotes — the force of hypocrisy
> and cultivated inattention combined with a certain
> minimum of alms.
>
> But there will be minds, and probably some
> powerful minds among them, who will go in quest of a
> morality more appropriate to the needs of the situation
> and permitting, within the situation, both honesty and
> a good conscience. Such minds may well turn to

Nietzsche, reading him, not in the gentle adaptations of Cold War scholarship, but for his bracing fierceness. There is much there for their comfort, not only in the general ethic, but also in specific applications. Nietzsche approves "Annihilation of decaying races." He also has this to say in *The Will to Power*: "The great majority of men have no right to existence, but are a misfortune to higher men. I do not yet grant the failures (*den Missrathenen*) the right. There are also peoples that are failures (*missrathene Volker*)."

Let me now comment, from the perspective of 1994, on the two main aspects of that 1970 scenario for the year 2000. I refer to the external aspect — the pressures from the poor world on the rich world — and the internal effect — the moral and ethical mutations within the rich world, in consequence of these pressures, and of other pressures.

In both those aspects, there are things which I foresaw, twenty-four years ago, and things which I did not. The things I did not foresee but begin to see now make the total picture significantly worse than what I did foresee.

First, the external pressures. At the present stage — near the middle of the last decade of the second millennium of the Christian Era — the pressures are mainly received in the form of attempted population movements and the curbing of those movements. The hands are on the sides of the boat, and the captain has the hatchets out. Poor people are trying to move North — out of Latin America towards the United

States, out of North Africa into Southern Europe. In Europe, poor people are also trying to move from East to West. So that Western Europe has two population frontiers to man, while the United States looks southward. Yet the United States also has greater powers of attraction, and the alarm of its authorities is at present even more manifest than fears in France and Germany.

The rhetoric of the United States towards the Third World — and especially towards Latin America — has emphasized the need to encourage the spread of democracy. But the cases of Cuba and Haiti, as handled in 1994 by the Clinton Administration, suggest that the United States is much less concerned with the spread of democracy than with having governments in the Caribbean (and no doubt in Latin America also) that will be able and willing to prevent their populations from migrating north.

The deal Clinton did with Fidel Castro in September 1994 was entirely based on a relaxation of anti-Cuban sanctions by the United States, in exchange for an undertaking by the Cuban dictator to prevent any further emigration of Cuban people to the United States. This remarkable deal is a complete reversal of what has hitherto been official policy towards Cuba. Under that former policy, those who left Cuba for the U.S. were freedom-loving people fleeing from an oppressive regime. Now the oppressive regime — which has hardly changed — is told, in practice, that it can be as oppressive as it likes, so long as it keeps those whom it is oppressing safely confined to Cuba. This major policy shift — which has not been seriously controversial in America — is a measure of how the prevention of any further mass emigration has risen, in practice, though not in rhetoric, to the top of the American political agenda.

The U.S. military intervention in Haiti that same month was conducted under sloganry of liberation: Operation Uphold Democracy and later Operation Restore Democracy. In fact, the intervention was triggered by the arrival in Florida of thousands of Haitian boat people, and the attempted or projected arrival of many thousands more. The object of the intervention was to ensure that a Haitian government would prevent any further mass emigration. Whether the Haitian government that will do this is or is not nominally headed by President Jean-Bertrand Aristide will make no substantial difference. The only Haitians who can keep other Haitians from emigrating are the Haitians whom the U.S. president was denouncing in the week before the intervention, and with some of whom he did a deal on the day before the intervention. That is to say, generically, the Haitian military leadership and, within that caste, those elements who know what side their bread is buttered on and will do what the Americans tell them in those matters which are of real concern to the Americans.

There are not many such matters in economically insignificant Haiti, and by far the most important of these is the prevention of mass emigration from Haiti to the U.S. If there were a genuine democracy in Haiti — a most improbable proposition — it would certainly vote for freedom of emigration. So Haiti may well get a democratic front, with President Aristide or another in nominal charge, but real power will remain with a favoured section of the Haitian military, because only the Haitian military, and its tried methods, can be relied on to prevent emigration north, the only real objective of Operation Restore Democracy.

When I wrote, in 1970, that "larger and larger doses of hypocrisy" would be required towards the end of the twentieth century, I didn't know the half of it. The year 1994 is a lot more like Orwell's *Nineteen Eighty-four* than the chronological 1984 was. Operation Restore Democracy is a masterpiece both of Newspeak and Doublethink.

The point I am making here is not an anti-American one. It is true that American levels of self-righteousness, and therefore of hypocrisy, are significantly higher than most Europeans can afford — although the British do pretty well in both lines, and so do the Irish, the latter with the agreeable sideline of being able to feel superior about the British variety of hypocrisy, which is more obvious at a distance than the Irish one. But whatever the variations in levels and styles of hypocrisy, all the affluent, and relatively affluent, countries are agreed about the basics: Keep out poor would-be immigrants.

We may be sure that the French, Spanish, and Italian governments are sending similar messages — in substance though not in form — to North African governments as the Americans send to the Caribbean, and that the Germans are sending the same message to the governments to the east of them. The message is:

"We'll do what we can to help you, provided you make sure to keep your people at home." And this policy has the support of the peoples of all the affluent and relatively affluent democracies. Any democratic government that decided to accept uncontrolled mass immigration of poor people would fall immediately.

So far, we in the affluent world are having things all our own way. But this cannot last. Things are getting worse out there in "the less developed world," as the current international jargon calls it, and they will continue to get worse, in a variety of ways, throughout at least the first century of the third millennium. The implications of the population figures are appalling, if we will just look at them instead of listening to sophists who do their best to make them sound harmless.

In 1970, when I wrote the article from which I have quoted here, the population of the world, according to the agreed international statistics, amounted to nearly four billion people. This year the population amounts to nearly six billion people. That is an increase of nearly two billion people in twenty-four years: an increase, that is, of about fifty percent.

The *rate* of increase has been slowly falling, but most of the slowing is in the population of the affluent countries. According to estimates made in early 1994, the population of "the less developed world" will *double* over the next thirty-six years. If the kind of measures approved at Cairo are actually put into effect, on a large scale, the doubling will take a bit longer, but probably not much longer. The slowing down of population growth is itself a frighteningly slow process, and the size of the population already there is so great that even small accretions, seen as a proportion of the whole, are extremely large, in absolute terms.

This represents an enormous increase in human misery and in human anger. The affluent countries — of whom you and I are part — can probably keep the misery at arm's length, as we are now doing, for a long time to come. But I think we may have increasing trouble with aggression from out there, as the next century progresses. In this connection the theories of the late Lin Piao may have some continuing relevance.

Lin Piao was an eminent Chinese Marxist theoretician, under Chairman Mao. He was later disgraced and liquidated under Mao's successors, but that of course neither validates nor invalidates his theories. He is best known for his theory of world revolution, around the concept of "the countrysides" versus "the cities." In the Chinese Revolution, the peasant-soldiers first made good their control of the countryside and then moved in on the cities, partly by starving them out. In Lin Piao's theory of world revolution, the Third World is the countryside, while the affluent areas are the cities. The cities will be forced to submit to the countryside throughout the world, following the Chinese model, previously established.

In the form proposed by Lin Piao, the theory lacks credibility: "the cities" of the affluent world, with their abundant stores of food, are not to be starved out by the Third World, much of which is itself on the verge of starvation and kept alive partly by Western contributions. Nor is actual military conquest of the West by the Third World even a remotely serious possibility. Yet his general idea has truth in it to this extent; that violent attacks out of the Third World, against Western targets, are likely to be on the increase throughout the next century, and perhaps for a longer period.

The attacks that have occurred so far have mainly come from Muslim sources: Iran, Libya, Syria, and various points in the ambiguous political nebula known as the PLO. The inveterate Muslim hostility to the infidel West may fluctuate in intensity, and vary in territorial incidence, but it is unlikely to go away, and will probably increase. Muslim fundamentalists will almost certainly grow in numbers, both as a proportion of the Muslim population and of Third World population. They are good at making converts, and also their rejection of artificial contraception will keep the fundamentalist fertility rate and birth rate at much higher — and increasingly higher — levels than those prevailing among their non-fundamentalist neighbours, let alone the affluent West.

Muslim hostility, therefore, is likely to increase in the course of the next century. But other kinds of terrorists are likely to arise, dominating their own districts, and then beginning to look for other worlds to conquer. Among the other worlds, by far the most attractive prospect is the affluent West.

People in the affluent countries are in the habit of thinking of the Third World poor as an undifferentiated mass. In reality, the Third World ghettoes — such as the townships of South Africa — are the centres of an intensified and accelerated process of natural selection, culminating in the creation of a particularly ferocious criminal elite. This should not surprise anyone. Where there are very few jobs, or almost no jobs, active youngsters are bound to turn to crime. And in such conditions, competition among criminals will be peculiarly intense. Those who rise to the top will be the toughest of the tough, the most ruthless among the cunning, the most cunning among the ruthless, and the angriest among the angry. A natural aristocracy indeed, and not so very different from the robber barons of the European Middle Ages and some later Western aristocracies, either in their origins or in their outlook and patterns of behaviour.

There are rising elites of that kind, not only in the Third World but in the great cities of the former Soviet Union, and even in the great cities of the West, especially in the ghettoes of cities like Los Angeles. These are predatory elites, formed for the acquisition of loot and power (as well as for the expression of anger), and it seems inevitable that sooner or later they will concentrate on the places where most of the loot and power are, the dominant sections of the the great cities of the West. Various combinations of groups of criminal elites — inside and outside the West — will be formed both for outright robbery, muscling in on existing rackets, such as the drug traffic, and for terrorist blackmail, including perhaps nuclear blackmail, with devices acquired from Russia. In any event, such groups will have no more difficulty than the IRA has had in getting their hands on large quantities of modern weaponry. And they may well find, as the IRA has found, that modern Western governments are a pretty soft touch when a combination of terror and blackmail is applied.

At the present stage of the eve of the millennium, terrorist assaults on Western targets from bases in the Third World are still rare, the attack by Muslim terrorists on the New York Trade Center being the prime example to date. The Third World pressures, in 1994, are felt mainly in the form of poor people trying to get in, and being kept out. In that sense, we have already reached the stage foreseen in that 1970 article, when I wrote: "The advanced world may well be like, and feel like, a closed and guarded palace, in a city gripped by the plague." The assault on the palace, out of the plague-gripped city, has yet to begin, but we can already sense its imminence.

Let us now turn to the ethical and intellectual implications of the stage we have now reached: the "closed and guarded palace," on the eve of the attack and of the millennium. In that essay, I did not yet foresee the kind of terrorist attacks I have been discussing, but I did get as far as the closed and guarded palace and its ethical and intellectual implications. As I wrote then:

> The traditional ethic will require larger and larger doses of its traditional built-in antidotes — the forces of hypocrisy and cultivated inattention combined with a certain minimum of alms.

I foresaw, in that essay, quite a lot about our present condition. But I confess that I did not foresee quite as large doses of hypocrisy and cultivated inattention as we ingested throughout the West as recently as the autumn of 1994. Operation Restore Democracy beats all previous records in the domain of hypocrisy, as have the responses of the media and the public to that operation, in the domain of cultivated inattention. In the American media in particular, most reporters and commentators have been describing and discussing the prospects for the restoration of democracy in Haiti as if democracy were a venerable Haitian institution, and as if Clinton were devoting his mind to its prospects in Haiti, at a time when it was perfectly obvious that his mind was exclusively concentrated on the prospects of the Democratic candidates in the mid-term Congressional elections. All that concerned the president about Haiti was *Haiti-as-an-electoral-issue*: that is, what Haiti can be made to look like to voters who neither know nor care about the real-life country. Haiti-as-an-issue is an affair of smoke, mirrors, and spin doctors. Real-life Haitians, in the shape of boat people, have to be kept out: out of the campaign and out of the country. Operation Restore Democracy was really Operation Return the Democratic Candidates. It may not have worked, but that was the idea; the *only* idea.

All these commentators, being as well-informed as you or I, know all this perfectly well, with one part of their minds. But when they write for publication, they think with another part of their mind: one which is

attuned to the elaboration of decorous fictions as reas-
suring substitutes for disreputable realities. (I am
speaking about most of the coverage and comment;
there are honourable exceptions.)

The central theme of this book, though often lying
under the surface, is the future of the mainstream Enlightenment tradition, which has been at the centre of
our Western culture throughout most of the second
half of the second millennium, now drawing to an end.
In that connection, I am more perturbed by the intellectual than the moral aspects of the phenomena we have
been discussing. The application of reason to the human
situation has been the *idée maîtresse* of the Enlightenment. But how can you apply reason to the human
situation if your cognitive processes have decayed, or
been debauched, to such an extent that you are being
presented, and are presenting yourself, with a falsified
picture of the human situation?

It seems to me that an alarmingly high proportion
of communicators, on the eve of the millennium, are
suffering from some sort of cognitive degeneration,
unless we assume that they are consciously lying,
which I don't believe to be the case. However that may
be, the picture of the world we live in that we are
receiving — through television, radio, and the press —
is a curious mixture of fact and fiction. The facts,
mostly in the form of pictures, are very often horrify-
ing. The fiction comes into the commentary and interpretation, heavily charged with wishful fantasy,
unwarranted reassurance, and intimations of quick
fixes. Democracy is being restored in Haiti. The horrors

of civil war in former Yugoslavia can be abolished by blowing up Serbs or arming Muslims.

Such distortions and illusions are not entirely a result of what may be called "the guarded palace syndrome." They are favoured by the state and tendency of the late-twentieth-century communications process: featuring very fast communications, a rapid sequence of varying sensational images, and very short attention spans. George Santayana seems to have had an intuition of the mental degenerate now getting in when he warned against "a mind without scope and without pause." (The phrase is part of an inscription in the dining room of Massey College.) These ominous features of the eve of the millennium all tend to aggravate the tendency to flinch from reality which is characteristic of the guarded palace syndrome.

The reality of the relations between the advanced world and the Third World has become such that it is natural for us to flinch from it. Yet when flinching from reality becomes habitual in the life of an individual, he is found to be insane. Too many among us, and among our opinion-formers in particular, are habitual flinchers in relation to Third World situations, and often in other ways also. The growing prevalence of this condition threatens the survival of Enlightenment values, and of the institutions derived from these. One of the many unpleasant possibilities that face us, who are the privileged inhabitants of an increasingly overcrowded planet, is that of a kind of collective madness. This could be the result of suppressed guilt — especially at the level of the best-informed members of our society — resulting eventually in a collective denial of reality.

That ghastly outcome is neither inevitable nor chimerical; it is a serious possibility which can be inferred — as a possibility, and no more — from existing tendencies at work in the advanced societies on the eve of the millennium. If we are to have hope of averting such an outcome, we need soon to begin to reverse the tendencies I have been considering: the tendencies which are making flinching from reality habitual in our culture.

To begin with, we need to do what a patient threatened with emotional and mental breakdown is most often advised to do. We need to dig up that buried guilt of ours and ascertain its extent and its limits. We need to find how much there is that we can do something about, and how much that we can do nothing to remove. Then we need to get on with doing what we can do, and get on also with living with conscious acceptance of that degree of guilt which is inseparable from our condition as the kind of people we are, in the kind of world we happen to live in. *Conscious* acceptance: we must rigorously deny ourselves the poisoned comfort of illusion, or we shall degenerate below the level of *homo sapiens* at some point in the course of the third millennium.

What we can do for the Third World is significant but quite limited. Most of the best work is being done by private agencies like Oxfam and Médicins sans Frontières. The Cairo agenda is critically important. But the best that can actually be done will not likely make more than a dent in the great and growing mess of human misery.

The first thing to feel clear about is that we do have a lot to feel guilty about. The second is that most of the guilt is inseparable from our condition.

We are actually in the position of the people in that lifeboat which I referred to earlier. Hands are clutching at the sides of the lifeboat, and the captain, with our acquiescence, is cutting off those hands to save our lives as well as his own. Such incidents have often happened in the history of seafaring. The survivors knew that they had really no sensible alternative. To allow all those desperate swimmers to swarm aboard would have sunk the boat, leaving those aboard it to perish along with the swimmers, doing no good at all to anyone. But that rational consideration can have done little to relieve the guilt of the survivors. Rational considerations do not penetrate dreams, or obliterate the image of a hatchet severing a wrist.

In our dreams, as in the dreams of our ancestors on the eve of the second millennium, there is a frolicsome demon, gaily whispering in our ear: "You're damned!"

We in the lifeboat of the advanced world don't actually see the hatchet. The job is done for us in as abstract and impersonal a way as possible, through immigration regulations and quotas. It is all a matter of routine, and so not covered by the media almost all of the time: we only get occasional glimpses of the reality, through the boat people — Vietnamese, Cuban, and Haitian. Once these are tidied out of the way — out of the way of cameras and a short attention span — the unobserved routine of exclusion sets in again.

Yet we know what is being done, and that it is done for our sake, and we approve of it, silently. The inner logic is the same as that of the lifeboat. Permitting mass immigration from the poor world would swamp our economies and our societies. We would drown in a sea of poverty, our immigrant poor would drown along with us — as would the poor already here — and the Third World would be no better off for the disappearance of the advanced world. In fact the Third World would be worse off from that disappearance; not enormously worse off, but significantly so.

Permission of mass immigration from the Third World to the advanced would actually not be to the advantage to the former. That can be demonstrated. But the demonstration is irrelevant, ethically speaking. We know, if we are honest with ourselves, that it is for our own sakes, not for theirs, that we are keeping all these people out. Of course there is a remedy for that knowledge, which is *not* to be honest with ourselves. Yet this remedy for guilt has a disastrous side effect, since it erodes the intellect.

That toxic remedy is always tempting to all of us, but it is especially seductive to Americans, for reasons which are in large part creditable to them. These reasons are deeply rooted in their history — going back to their country's seventeenth-century Puritan roots. Americans like to think of their country as ethically motivated, unlike the countries of the Old World, which are motivated by *realpolitik*. This ethically ambitious posture has had some large benign effects, as in the abolition of slavery in the nineteenth century, and the abolition of institutions of racial oppression in the twentieth. Yet the assumption of ethical superiority can also have extremely deleterious effects, especially in the field of foreign policy. It can lead to the ingestion of dangerously large doses of hypocrisy and cultivated inattention. It *has* led, and very recently, to the general acceptance, at face value, of Operation Restore Democracy.

That way madness lies, quite literally. If that level of wishful fantasy should become the norm, and should then perhaps even be surpassed, our whole Western culture will be going out of its collective mind, probably within the first quarter of the third millennium.

I spoke just now of an affliction threatening our whole Western culture, yet the specific phenomenon I had been considering — let us call it the ethical imperative — is peculiar to America, not general to the West. The French national heritage, since Richelieu's day, is rich in cynicism, especially in its inherently distasteful relations with the dim non-Francophone world. The rich Italian political imagination, shaped by Machiavelli, proudly dispenses with an ethical dimension. The German case is necessarily more complex, because of that ghastly fracture line across their history from the second to the fifth decade of the twentieth century. *Realpolitik* is a German word and was the governing concept of the foreign policies both of Imperial Germany and the Third Reich. Since 1945, successive German governments dutifully repudiated *realpolitik* and echoed American ethical rhetoric. The same is true of Japan. But in both cases one somehow senses a lack of enthusiasm, an absence of internal commitment to a value system adopted as a result of external constraints. There are times when *realpolitik* itself requires a repudiation of *realpolitik*. The prince, as Machiavelli said, must cultivate an appearance of piety. Real piety, on the other hand, is apt to get in the way.

Of all the Western countries — except perhaps Canada — Britain best understands the American ethical imperative, for this derives initially from the Puritan part of Britain's own past. There have been no more ardent exponents of the ethical imperative than Oliver Cromwell and William Ewart Gladstone. But there were also many Britons who distrusted and detested Cromwell in the seventeenth century, and Gladstone in the nineteenth.

Both Britain and the United States have known the ethical imperative, but the resistance to it is much more marked in the British tradition than in the American. Gladstone, in his time, was blamed less for having the ace of trumps up his sleeve than for claiming that Almighty God had put it there. Many Britons feel the same way, only more so, about the ethical dimension in the formulation of American foreign policy. The "more so" is supplied by nationalist sentiment. It is one thing to hear a national leader of one's own identifying the eternal principles of morality with the national interests of one's own nation. It is another to hear the national leader of *another* nation — even one's closest ally — effortlessly and fluently making the same identification, on behalf of that nation. British diplomats, constantly exposed to American political-ethical rhetoric, find their professional skills tested to the limits by the need to keep a straight face. For illustrations of what I mean, study the photographs of the expressions worn by Mr. Douglas Hurd at any international conference involving all the Western allies.

It is healthy, up to a point, that there should be an element of cynicism in the responses of America's allies to the American ethical imperative as a force in international politics. The allies need to be able to decode formulations whose real practical meaning often does not lie on the surface. That decoding requires an element of cynicism in the framing of hypotheses, and when the decoding is complete, the results may tend to increase the initial cynicism. Yet it is important to keep this partly salutary cynicism within limits. In the inter-relations of Western countries, solidarity should genuinely take precedence over reservations and cynical interpretations. We are all in the same boat even if — or rather, especially as — we have reason to feel uneasy about the ways in which our boat has to be kept afloat.

What is most important about the United States, for the rest of the West, is not that it is the richest and most powerful of the Western countries, nor that it is the leader of a military alliance, whose precise purposes, at the present moment in history, are not altogether clear. What is of primary importance is that the U.S. is the heart and soul of the Western value system, the Enlightenment tradition, which sustains and permeates the Western institutional framework of democracy, freedom of expression, and the rule of law.

The United States is the heart and soul of the Enlightenment tradition, not just because it is the richest and most powerful of the countries belonging within (or converted to) that tradition, but also because it is the only country committed to the Enlightenment tradition *emotionally as well as intellectually*. That tradition is part and parcel of the American civil religion. The Declaration of Independence and the Constitution of the United States are both Enlightenment documents, and also (paradoxically) sacred documents of the American civil religion. Religion and nationalism, which in other countries are always potential and often actual enemies of the Enlightenment, have in America been bound together with it, ever since the country itself came into being.

No other major Western country comes close to the U.S. in its commitment to the Enlightenment tradition. Britain comes nearest, of course, but still not very near, although it was in Britain that the Enlightenment first took institutional forms, in the Glorious Revolution of 1688. To measure the gap between the two commitments, compare the celebrations of the bicentenary of the Declaration of Independence, in 1976, and of the tercentenary of the Glorious Revolution, in 1988. The United States celebrated its bicentenary with loving pride and pomp and ceremony. The British, on the other hand, commemorated 1688 in a muted and embarrassed manner, as if they did not wish to offend the Jacobites.

It is true that the French, in the year following the muffled British tercentenary, did celebrate the bicentenary of *their* revolution with considerable external *éclat* and panache. As it happens I was in Paris for that July 14. It was a splendid party, but essentially a wake. The specifically French Enlightenment tradition, descending to posterity as the cult of the French Revolution, turned into Communism, both in France and Russia, and the modern French don't want to know about it. The 1989 celebrations, presided over by President Mitterrand, were actually a celebration of a particular document of 1789, which had remained inoperative throughout the entire course of the French Revolution. The document is the *Déclaration des droits de l'homme et du Citoyen* of August of that year. This happens to be a document of mainly American inspiration. Thomas Jefferson, who was minister plenipotentiary of the United States in Paris at the time, took the leading part in the composition of the French *Déclaration des droits*, as he had in the composition of a more influential Declaration thirteen years before. Modern France is not connected with the Enlightenment, through an indigenous tradition sustained throughout the two hundred years plus of its own ideologically chequered history since the French Revolution. France, as a nation-state, fully adhered to the Enlightenment only after the Second World War, and this was and is an Enlightenment tradition of mainly English-speaking inspiration, now most securely established in the United States.

The more we look at the connection between the Enlightenment and the major Western powers, the more we see, I think, that the continued predominance of the Enlightenment tradition in the West depends on its continued predominance in the United States.

I should now like to take a deep breath, and project myself in imagination into the middle of the next millennium. What forces, known to us on the eve of that millennium, would we expect to find still at work five hundred years from now?

I would feel fairly sure of finding religion and nationalism still there, in various forms, for the rather mechanical reason that they have already been around for a very long time: they have demonstrated durability of a high order. The durability would be universally conceded in the case of religion, but some may well wonder about nationalism. Nationalism is generally considered to be a phenomenon of fairly recent origin; many textbooks date it from the late eighteenth century, either just before or just after the French Revolution. I think this is an error in categorization. What happened in the late eighteenth century was not that nationalism came into existence for the first time. What happened was nationalism's sudden severance from something from which it had felt itself to be inseparable over millennia. That something was religion. Religion and nationalism are conjoined in both the root-systems of our Judaeo-Hellenic culture. They are present in the Hebrew Bible (*aka* the Old Testament) in the governing concepts of a Chosen People and a Promised Land. They are present in Ancient Hellas and Ancient Rome in the form of the bonding religious cults of those who died for the *polis* and the *patria*.

From the late eighteenth century on, nationalism emerges as a force on its own, conceptually speaking, but still invested with a very strong emotional aura closely resembling that which had belonged to the ancient amalgam of religion and nationalism. It might not be very wide of the mark to think of nationalism as a development *within* religion, a development emphasizing the earth rather than the sky: pushing what had been a *tendency* within Christianity since the Middle Ages towards a more-or-less logical conclusion.

In the immediate present context, all I am concerned to do is to show the antiquity of both religion and nationalism. Both have demonstrated staying power: they have commanded the allegiance of millions of human beings continuously over millennia and throughout our planet. It is natural — though not logically coercive — to assume that they can take another half-millennium more or less in their stride.

The Enlightenment tradition appears as less securely established. It has indeed been with us for a very long time, even though often in compromise with or submissive to various forms of religion and of nationalism. In Plato's Socratic dialogues, written down about the middle of the last millennium before the Christian Era, we today can recognize the spirit of what came, long, long after Socrates and Plato, to be called the Enlightenment. Throughout the intervening years there were some people marked by that spirit, in every generation. But it wasn't until the late-seventeenth and eighteenth centuries that Enlightenment ideas came to be the kind of major force in social and political life that religion and nationalism had been for millennia, and still are. The late emergence of Enlightenment as a force in history is one of the reasons for wondering whether the Enlightenment tradition can survive into, say, the second half of the third millennium.

There is another reason for doubting the durability of the Enlightenment which may seem more compelling to many, in the late twentieth century. Whereas religion and nationalism have always attracted masses of people, the Enlightenment tradition has always been one of elites: more precisely, of an intellectual elite, within a social elite. Socrates was the most notorious elitist of his day, a blasphemer both against the Olympian gods and the people of Athens (which really amounted to the same thing).

Much later, at the beginning of the modern age, in the English Glorious Revolution and in the American Revolution, elites permeated by Enlightenment values were carried to power almost by accident (as far as the Enlightenment connection was concerned). The English Whigs and the American revolutionaries had mass support, and the support of the Protestant pulpits, because they were the most efficient and successful exponents of the national will, which was then the will, in both cases, of a Protestant nation.

But what the masses did not know was that in both cases their revolutionary heroes were children of the Enlightenment, as sceptical about the literal inspiration of the Bible as they were contemptuous of papist dogmas and practices. The masses of that time didn't know about Enlightenment. The word itself would still not be widely understood, although values derived from it — particularly religious tolerance — are quite widespread. Still, understanding of the Enlightenment tradition and commitment to it are necessarily confined to elites, even if rather wide elites. And it is understandable that this should be so. Unlike religion and nationalism, the Enlightenment tradition has little or no emotive power. That in itself must make us fear for its capacity to survive through the first centuries of the coming millennium.

More ominous still, perhaps, is the fact that negative emotions are now being aroused against the whole culture and civilization which have grown up under the influence of the Enlightenment over the past three hundred years or so. This arousal is being conducted through the medium of that fascinating late development of Orwellian Newspeak which is known as "politically correct." In the limited but highly charged vocabulary of the politically correct, no term is more comprehensively damning than "elitist." The term "racist" is more emotionally fraught, but "racism" is thought of as a form of "elitism," and those who defend the existence and legitimacy of *any* kind of elite can plausibly be branded as condoning racism, and can therefore be exposed as morally dead. Historically, the Enlightenment tradition is demonstrably an affair of elites, and therefore "politically correct" is inherently hostile to the Enlightenment tradition and is a significant recruit to the forces that threaten the survival of that tradition.

"Politically correct" and multiculturalism — PCM for short — are not so much allies as different aspects of the same levelling enterprise, now being conducted, with menacing enthusiasm, on many American and other campuses. For the most fervent of the multiculturalists, the enemy is nothing less than Western culture in all its aspects. "Hey ho, hey ho, Western culture's got to go" is a jingle which has been heard from students at Stanford University, and no doubt on many other campuses as well. If this was just student high spirits it would be harmless, and could even be healthy; a bit of irreverence would have been all to the good back in the 1950s when the Ivy League campuses and other upmarket campuses like Stanford were treating Western culture with excessive and uncritical deference (as some liberal commentators still do). But this is something different. In the 1990s, students who chant "Western culture's got to go" are not challenging values uncritically professed by their instructors. They are actually *echoing* values uncritically professed by their instructors. Not all their instructors, no doubt, but the ones whose value judgements they accept and who have the most influence with them.

So fine: Where do we go from there? Western culture's got to go. Agreed, for the sake of argument. But what then? What do we put in its place? Multiculturalism? Hardly. Most of these students, and most of the teachers whom they admire and follow, know no language other than English, and have no serious intention of learning any. The departments in which multiculturalism is most cherished, on almost all

American campuses, are the departments of English. These people, both instructors and students, *have* no culture other than Western culture in its specifically American forms, as modified by late twentieth-century fashions. When these people say "Western culture's got to go," they are calling for the departure of the only culture they actually have. This is much worse even than nineteenth-century know-nothingism. It is a form of cultural self-castration. "These old things are no use to me! Why don't we cut them off? Western culture's got to go!"

Multiculturalism in its aspect as the rejection of the only culture one actually has is parallelled by another aspect of PCM: populism without a people. PCM is nothing if not anti-elitist. And again it turns out to be nothing, period, being the rejection of itself. The seats of learning where PCM is now most securely established include most of the elite academies of America: in the east, Harvard, Yale, Princeton, and Duke; in the west, Stanford and Berkeley. Those of the products of those institutions who have imbibed politically correct values — not a majority of these products but a significant minority — project these values into the ethos of the wider middle class, and a large part of the media. The discourse of the working class remains politically incorrect and even scandalously so.

PCM, along with post-structuralism, deconstruction, and similar intellectual delights, is strictly elite stuff. But that does nothing to lessen our concern for the future of the Enlightenment tradition, for it is by and through elites that that has been carried from generation to generation. If a significant part of the American academic elite rejects or thinks it is rejecting the whole of Western culture, then the chances of the survival of the Enlightenment tradition are thereby significantly reduced proportionately.

Or at least they would be significantly reduced if we assume that PCM and its ideological accomplices will continue to be influential up to, say, the end of the next century. If they do — or if other levelling fads from the same stable take over from them — then I fear that the condition of the Enlightenment tradition may prove terminal within, say, the first quarter of the next millennium. But we need not, at this stage, make such a dire assumption. There are some signs that reason may be beginning to reassert itself, even in the worst-afflicted sectors of American academia.

It is relevant to note here that PCM is itself a product of the Enlightenment tradition, like so much else that has come to threaten that tradition in our time. Enlightenment values were at the heart of abolitionism. And *women* abolitionists were the founders of American feminism: the first serious feminist movement in the world. From the middle of the nineteenth century the movement for racial equality and the movement for gender equality were associated. Not always harmoniously; there has often been friction between them. But they were joined — despite the objections of some white women and some black men — by the inner logic of Enlightenment values: *for* equality of opportunity and *against* arbitrary exclusions based on unverified ascription of inferiority to large categories of human beings.

As a result, in large part, of these great Enlightenment movements operating over more than a century, the position of both women and blacks
improved to such an extent that, by the late twentieth
century, considerable numbers of both groups were
faculty members as well as students in major universities. At this point, an understandable but regretta-
ble informal coalition came into being between the
two categories of the formerly excluded. Coalitions
are always directed against someone, and this one
was directed against white males: dead white males
and live white males. This adversarial coalition was
at the origin of, and is still at the core of, the negative
multiculturalist agenda culminating in "Western
culture's got to go."

It seems increasingly likely, however, that multiculturalism may have to go before Western culture has
to. There are signs that the multiculturalist alliance is
under stress. In particular, and somewhat unexpect-
edly, the rising influence of black feminism within the
general feminist movement — although it has been
favoured and accredited by the prestige of multiculturalism — tends, on the whole, to undermine the
multiculturalist alliances on the campuses. Black feminists do not indeed admire white males as much as
white males admire themselves, but neither are black
feminists disposed to view white males, living or dead,
as the *sole* villains of the piece, sole oppressors of blacks
and women. Black feminists are aware that it is not
only white *males* who are racists: white females have
often been so and often still are. Black feminists also

know that it is not only *white* males who are sexists: black males have often been so and often still are. Black feminists are probably the biggest challenge to PCM but not the only one. It seems to me that the black male students and the white female students of today are less preoccupied with the peculiar wickedness of the white male than was the case of many of their predecessors in the previous decade. All in all there seems to be a fair chance that PCM may fade out during the first quarter of the next century.

It may, if we assume that PCM, as we now know it, is an isolated phenomenon and not a symptom of a wider malaise in Western society. I fear it may be a symptom of a wider degeneration within the Western mind, and related to other symptoms, such as those indicative of deep malaise within the democratic system. I spoke earlier of an *inherent* weakness in democracy: the tendency to produce — except in occasional extraordinary circumstances — leaders who are specialists in winning popularity contests. Whether they have any other admirable qualities is largely a matter of luck. Full democracy — with women voting as well as men — is less than a hundred years old. It has had an adequate run of luck so far, but the luck may be beginning to run out along with the twentieth century and the second millennium.

One large source of the present trouble is that modern communications are working on that inherent weakness in ways that may be transforming it into a terminal pathological condition. In the late twentieth century, issues tend to be defined by television images, to which speedy responses must be improvised, without either the public or the governing respondents having more than a hazy notion of the context of the images, or of what might constitute an appropriate response to the actual situation of which the fleeting image is necessarily an inadequate exposé. In practice, the success or failure of the response is not defined by its effects on that situation but by opinion polls and popularity ratings. Democracy is turning into a series of instant plebiscites, over which the spin doctor is king. There is a tragic paradox here in that the forms which freedom of expression is taking in the late twentieth century are beginning to threaten democracy itself: the only tradition that permits freedom of expression.

In international policy-forming especially and within the guarded palace syndrome, the instant plebiscites, manipulated by the spin doctors, tend to manufacture a fantasy world, as recently exemplified in the charade Operation Restore Democracy. Such charades are designed to deceive the masses and win elections. But the most ominous feature of this process, as far as the future of the Enlightenment tradition is concerned, is the degree of acceptability which such a charade can command among the intellectual elite of the communications world. At the beginning of October 1994, Anthony Lewis, the resident liberal pundit of the *New York Times*, called Operation Restore Democracy "amazingly successful." "Now it is time," he wrote, "for pride at a job being well done."

A bad case there of late-twentieth-century intellectual dry rot.

The symptoms of democracy getting out of control are more obvious in the United States than elsewhere in the West. Yet the United States possesses also more recuperative power. There and there alone, the Enlightenment tradition is interwoven with national pride and a civil religion, and has emotional appeal, and the stamina that goes with this combination. In some European countries the disease already looks like being terminal. Italy, where Fascism began, shows signs of returning to it. From France a simultaneous loss of confidence in *all* the democratic parties is reported. In Austria recently the far right has made staggering electoral gains. So far, neo-Nazism is weak in Germany, but if Fascism, in some form, should take over in Austria as well as in Italy, many Germans will be disposed to move in the same direction. Fascism, like its ancestor Nietzscheanism, is unfortunately an appropriate ideology for a guarded palace in a city gripped by the plague.

I have chosen to end on a sombre note, both because this is warranted and because I believe alarmism to be far less dangerous to us, in the late twentieth century, than the witless complacency which set in at the end of the Cold War.

I want to quote in conclusion a passage in which Friedrich Nietzsche, in 1887, looked forward to the next century: our own. But first a necessary word of interpretation about "God is dead" and about Nietzschean "cheerfulness."

By "God is dead," Nietzsche intended the reversal of the Christian ethic, based on compassion, which had survived the decline of revealed religion and animated the Enlightenment tradition. The "cheerfulness" he experienced as he looked ahead into the shadows of the coming century was about the imminent triumph of the principle he laid down in *The Will to Power*: "The great majority of men have no right to existence, but are a misfortune to higher men."

Looking forward in that spirit, Nietzsche wrote in Book V of *The Gay Science*:

> *The background of our cheerfulness*: The greatest recent event — that "God is dead," that the belief in the Christian God has ceased to be believable — is even now beginning to cast its first shadows over Europe. For the few, at least, whose eyes, whose suspicion in their eyes, is strong and sensitive enough for this spectacle, some sun seems to have set just now. . . . In the main, however, this may be said: the event itself is much too great, too distant, too far from the comprehension of the many even for the tidings of it to be thought of as having arrived yet, not to speak of the notion that many people might know what has really happened here, and what must collapse now that this belief has been undermined — all that was built upon it, leaned on it, grew into it; for example, our whole European morality. . . .
>
> Even we born guessers of riddles who are, as it were, waiting on the mountains, put there between today and tomorrow, we firstlings and premature births of the coming century, to whom the shadows that must soon envelop Europe really *should* have

appeared by now — why is it that even we look forward to it without any real compassion for this darkening, and above all without any worry and fear for *ourselves*? Is it perhaps that we are still too deeply impressed by the first consequences of this event — and these first consequences, the consequences for us, are perhaps the reverse of what one might expect: not at all sad and dark, but rather like a new, scarcely describable kind of light, happiness, relief, exhilaration, encouragement, dawn?

Indeed, we philosophers and "free spirits" feel as if a new dawn were shining on us when we receive the tidings that "the old god is dead"; our heart overflows with gratitude, amazement, anticipation, expectation. At last the horizon appears free again to us, even granted that it is not bright; at last our ships may venture out again, venture out to face any danger; all the daring of the lover of knowledge is permitted again; the sea, *our* sea, lies open again; perhaps there has never yet been such an "open sea."

"The shadows that must soon envelope Europe," as foreseen by Nietzsche, included Nazism, which was to acknowledge its debt to Nietzsche and his ethical revolution.

A disciple of Nietzsche looking forward into the shadows of the coming millennium might well experience that sinister Nietzschean "cheerfulness."

As the rest of us look towards the coming millennium we should be aware of the possibility of a return of the shadows. The millennium, therefore, should be an occasion for self-questioning, for rational apprehension, above all for trying to clear our heads, before it is too late. The prescription of a member of the British Millennium Commission — to celebrate the millennium with "fizz, panache, excitement" — is a recipe for passing away in a befuddled condition. Trivialization is not necessarily the most trivial of the combination of maladies from which our culture can die. And ingrowing triviality, the pompous frivolity of complacent Establishments, has been known to prepare the way for the emergence of ferocious new elites. That is among the possibilities for even the early part of the new millenium.

Acknowledgements

Thanks to Ann Saddlemyer, Master of Massey College, University of Toronto, my kind and outstanding host throughout the period of the recording of these lectures, my public lecture at Massey College, and accompanying activities. Thanks to David Wilson of the St. Michael's Celtic Studies Programme, who steered me so agreeably through Toronto, both in the literal and metaphorical sense. Thanks to the remarkable *Ideas* group at CBC, notably Lister Sinclair, Bernie Lucht, Peter Kavanagh, David Cayley, and Alison Moss, and to senior managers Alex Frame and Beth Haddon.

All the above made my stay in Toronto, in connection with the Massey Lectures, not only most enjoyable but also a memorable and enriching intellectual experience.

Thanks also to Bob Connor and the fellows and staff of the National Center for the Humanities in North Carolina and to Charles Blitzer and the fellows and staff of the Wilson Center in Washington, D.C. Several of the themes of these lectures developed in the stimulating intellectual environment provided by these two centres.

For the actual content of these lectures, and for anything anyone may find objectionable in any of them, I personally am of course solely responsible.

CONOR CRUISE O'BRIEN

ABOUT THE AUTHOR

Conor Cruise O'Brien is a distinguished statesman and writer. Over a long and varied career, he has served in the Irish external affairs office; was a member of the Irish delegation to the United Nations (at one point being seconded as a special assistant to UN Secretary General Dag Hammarskjöld); was elected an Irish Labour Party parliamentarian, later serving in the cabinet; and was appointed editor-in-chief of the *London Observer*. A contributing editor to *The Atlantic Monthly*, O'Brien lectures around the world at leading universities and writes weekly columns for *The Independent* in Britain and *The Irish Independent*. His many books include *States of Ireland* and *The Great Melody: A Thematic Biography of Edmund Burke*.